BILBERRY
A Seed in Good Soil

**The History of Bilberry Creek Baptist Church.
Its First Twenty-five Years (1984-2009)**

By: Gunter and Reinhilde Rochow

Published by Waldo Rochow
Cover by Waldo Rochow

Website: http://bilberry.rochow.info

ISBN: 978-1-926469-10-2 (*full colour*)
ISBN: 978-1-926469-11-9 (*black and white*)
ISBN: 978-1-926469-12-6 (*digital*)
First Edition

*"Still other seed fell on good soil, where it produced a crop –
a hundred, sixty or thirty times what was sown."*
Matthew 13:8 (NIV)

CONTENTS

BILBERRY – *A Seed in Good Soil*

FOREWORD BY THE REVEREND DON COLLAR

It is an honour for me to write the Foreword to this account of the first 25 years of ministry at Bilberry Creek Baptist Church and how it has sought to carry out its mission of "glorifying God and making and nurturing disciples."

I would like to express a special thanks to Gunter and Reinhilde Rochow, founding members and editors extraordinaire for the hundreds of hours they have dedicated to compiling this record of 25 years of service "making and nurturing disciples". In addition, I would like to give a heartfelt thank you to the many volunteers who willingly shared their memories of ministry.

The account is one of faithful Christians dreaming big dreams and prayerfully trusting God to make them happen. It's a story of "God's work; our hands."

With this publication, it is my hope that those who call Bilberry their church home today, and those who will come afterward will be inspired to continue to carry on their work for the Lord.

It has been a pleasure to have been its pastor for these 25 years. I have witnessed God at work in and among His people. I remember vividly the day when God called me to Bilberry. When I met with the Ottawa Baptist Association's steering committee to be interviewed for the job of pastor, I remember distinctly that I did not meet many of their predetermined requirements. However, from that first interview, we were all overwhelmed with a sense of God's call for my family to come to Orleans.

God drew faithful workers to Bilberry with gifts for ministry that I lacked and together Christ built His church. Together, we witnessed amazing answers to prayer.

With God's help, we forged an alliance between Bilberry and our French-speaking brothers and sisters at *Église Evangelique Baptiste d'Ottawa* to share the same facility so that together we could impact Orleans with the gospel in both official languages.

Throughout my years of ministry at Bilberry, the church family has encouraged me to play a broader pastoral role within the community. I have been privileged to serve as chaplain within the Canadian Armed Forces Primary Reserve and chaplain of Orleans Branch 632 of the Royal Canadian Legion. It has been an honour to share in people's joys and sorrows, victories as well as defeats.

The work of the church is never finished. There are more hearts to be touched by the gospel. There are more lives to be transformed by the love of Christ. There is much more to be done in God's kingdom.

Centuries ago, Teresa of Avila aptly wrote: "Christ has no body now on earth but yours, no hands but yours, no feet but yours; Yours are the eyes through which to look out at Christ's compassion to the world; Yours are the feet with which he is to go about doing good; Yours are the hands with which he is to bless men now." As the church moves forward, Bilberry will continue to be Christ's hands and feet in Orleans.

With the Apostle Paul, my prayer is: *"May God Himself, the God of peace, sanctify you through and through. May your whole spirit, soul and body be kept blameless at the coming of our Lord Jesus Christ. The One who calls you is faithful, and He will do it."*
(1 Thessalonians 5:23, 24)

May Bilberry's future be as bright and blessed as our past.

Don Collar

BILBERRY – *A Seed in Good Soil*

FOREWORD BY THE REVEREND NEIL HUNTER

In the spring of 1984, I went way out to Orleans to make a routine pastoral visit to one of the families of Bethany Baptist Church, where I was the Pastor. I drove around and around the streets of this growing community looking for the street where this family lived. As I drove, I said to myself, 'This is a BIG community. We need to plant a church here in Orleans'.

But, what to do? I decided to meet with Rev. George Cawfield, the former Pastor of Kanata Baptist Church. As we talked, I asked him the question, "As the founding Pastor of Kanata Baptist Church, what was done right and what was done wrong in establishing a new work in Kanata? His response was very enlightening and very helpful and we decided to move forward with the possibility of establishing a church in Orleans. We made three strategic decisions.

1.   We decided to go to the Ottawa Baptist Ministerial for their reflection and ultimately their support. Both of these things happened and we received its overwhelming support. The ministers also agreed to discuss this new work in their respective congregations in order, we hoped, to provide names of people who lived in Orleans who may be interested in being part of a new congregation.

2.   We took this Baptist Ministerial proposal to the Annual Meeting of the Ottawa Baptist Association in May of 1984. After an informative discussion, the Association voted to support a new work in Orleans. We did not specifically request financial support. At that time we did not know what kind of support we might require.

3.   With the unqualified support of both the Ministerial and the Association, we decided to form a Support and Steering Committee to begin the process of establishing a church in Orleans. With the excellent co-operation of local pastors, we secured representatives from Bethany, Eastview, First, McPhail, and Pleasant Park to form this very important and enthusiastic Committee. One thing George Cawfield did point out was the lack of support from existing Ottawa churches when he came to Ottawa to start the new work in Kanata in 1975. This time it was an Ottawa Baptist Association initiative with the blessing of local pastors.

Rev. Bert DeRoo, then Pastor of the Eastview Baptist Church, was elected as Chair and we held our first meeting in June 1984 at Eastview. Our second meeting, in July, more of a party and celebration, was held at the home of Gunter and Reinhilde Rochow. At this meeting, we really came together as a committee and we worked at assigning responsibilities to the committee members. The most important items on that agenda were: when do we start, what time of the day, and where would we begin our new outreach ministry in

Orleans. Even though in hindsight it all seemed to be rather straightforward, we did recognize that this was a daunting task that we had set for ourselves.

As the church history bears out, the first worship service for the then unnamed church was on Sunday, September 23 at 6:30 p.m. at Dunning-Foubert School on Prestwick Drive. The excitement was palpable as we met on that cool September evening. Bethany supplied the printed Order of Service and Gunter was our preacher.

At one of our meetings, we were looking for a name for this church and it was pointed out that Bilberry Creek flowed near (or was it under?) Dunning-Foubert School. So, in a rather unusual, almost playful way, we arrived at a name for this new outreach work. As the committee continued to meet in the homes of our committee members, most of whom were residents of Orleans, we looked at finances, ministry, programming and the calling of the first pastor.

My thanks go to all the members of that founding committee for their joy, commitment and tenacity, and to Rev. Bud Hooper, Associate Secretary of the Department of Canadian Missions of the Baptist Convention of Ontario and Quebec for his continuing support of our efforts and his helpfulness in the planting and calling process during the Fall of 1984 and the Winter of 1985, leading up to the calling and arrival of Bilberry's first Pastor, Rev. Don Collar, on Easter, 1985.

Respectfully submitted as one of the members of the Support and Steering Committee… and a continuing friend of Bilberry Creek Baptist Church.

Neil Hunter

PREFACE AND ACKNOWLEDGEMENTS

The purpose of writing any history is not only to gain retrospective insights, but also prospective guidance based on what we have learned from the past. To be valid, both aspects must be based on facts and their interpretation. In researching and writing the history of the first 25 years of Bilberry Creek Baptist Church, we have relied primarily on documents and statistics to the extent that these were available, as well as on interviews with knowledgeable persons. In particular, we wanted to hear the many experiences of the members and adherents of the congregation who invested so much of themselves in this ministry of love, so that later leaders can draw on, and adapt, that experience, as they lead the congregation forward. We, as writers, as well as the people who participated in data collection or were interviewed, were eyewitnesses of the unfolding ministry of *Bilberry Creek Baptist Church*. Nevertheless, we were surprised that over the relatively short period of twenty-five years, certain critical documents were nowhere to be found and that the recollections of some eye witnesses regarding particular events varied with respect to some details.[1]

In writing this history we refrained from producing a chronological "travelogue" of our twenty-five year journey as a congregation. Instead we chose a thematic approach that spans the entire period. In doing so, we could conveniently focus on the planning phase for ministry (Part 1), on the dimensions of ministry (Part 2), and on the interpretation of past experience and outlook to the future (Part 3). The planning for ministry in Part 1 began during the first fall and winter and continued throughout the entire period, as needed, including the organization of the congregation, the partnership with *Église Évangélique Baptiste d'Orléans*, and the first phase of the construction of our own place of worship.

> "Churches … must dig into their history to rediscover the dreams of their founding members. This process may be especially important for churches that are in transition between lead ministers."
>
> Robert Dale. *To Dream Again: How to Help Your Church Come Alive*

The dimension of ministry in Part 2 follows the Biblical types of ministry that were reflected in the original five administrative Commissions of the church, i.e.: (1) Worship; (2) Preaching, Mission and Evangelism; (3) Teaching; (4) Fellowship; and (5) Service. Needless, to say, many activities undertaken by the congregation transcended one or more of these forms of ministry. For instance, while the work of the Sunday School focused on teaching, it also contained elements of worship, evangelism and fellowship. Nevertheless, for the purposes of this history, structuring the Ministry of the church by these five broad types has more advantages than disadvantages.

In Part 3, we step back a bit and ask ourselves what we have learned as a congregation, and how that learning can help us in strengthening our ministry, as we look ahead into the next period of our congregational life.

Since the history of a congregation is an account of what God has done through his people, we have made an effort to tell some of that work through a selection of pictures that have been accumulated over the years.

In some cases, we found unique and significant documents or experiences that we attempted to preserve in a more complete format. To do so, we made use of free-standing text boxes. Other significant historical material has been presented in the form of appendices.

In writing this history, we have attempted to show, in form of a story, what God has done in our midst. Nevertheless, since we intended this to be an evidence-based history, we have chosen to use endnotes that will allow current members and future writers of history to return to the sources as they try to understand better the full picture or only parts of it.

We wish to acknowledge the valuable help which we have received from many of our members. Some of them helped us to find necessary documents, others expressed their willingness to be interviewed or to interview, and still others participated in other forms of data gathering, as well as by providing other support, such as reviewing the draft text with a view to identifying inaccuracies or significant gaps. Our son, Waldo Rochow, designed the title page, formatted the document for publication and managed the publication process.

Nevertheless, as this first edition of BCBC's history goes out, the readers may become aware of inadvertent inaccuracies or omissions, particularly if they involve people who should have been named. Therefore, we invite all readers to draw our attention to any such aspects in the hope that these can be reflected in a second edition, if one should be produced.

Gunter and Reinhilde Rochow
Ottawa, Canada
December 6, 2014

PART I: PLANNING FOR MINISTRY

BILBERRY – *A Seed in Good Soil*

Chapter 1: Organizing for Ministry

The starting point for *Bilberry Creek Baptist Church* (BCBC) goes back to church extension initiatives undertaken by the *Ottawa Baptist Association* (OBA) in the mid-1970s and the early 1980s. In the mid-1970s, Mark Parent, then a Pre-Divinity student, was engaged for the summer months to undertake a study in collaboration with a committee of representatives of existing Ottawa churches. His report was presented to the Reverend Archie Goldie, then the head of the *Department of Home Mission* of the *Baptist Convention of Ontario and Quebec* (BCOQ), now known as *Canadian Baptists of Ontario and Quebec* (CBOQ). Gunter Rochow was the representative for *First Baptist Church* on the OBA committee. The committee looked at opportunities for church extension in Orleans, Nepean and Barrhaven, as well as Kanata. In particular, Mark Parent undertook a canvass of the Kanata community and identified several families who were interested in becoming part of a new Baptist church. Thus, it was recommended that Kanata be chosen for the establishment of a new church and that the other locations be revisited at a later time.

Several years later, in the early 1980s, on the encouragement by the Reverend Neil Hunter, then the pastor of *Bethany Baptist Church*, the *Ottawa Baptist Association* reconvened its church extension committee, of which Gunter Rochow was again the representative for *First Baptist Church*. This time, the committee was given the mandate to look, in particular, at opportunities for church planting in the Orleans area. When the decision was made to proceed with church planting in Orleans, the existing Ottawa Baptist churches were encouraged to suggest to their members who lived in the Orleans area to consider becoming members of the new congregation. Six families responded to the "Macedonian call"[2] : They were the Jen, Kiar, Maitland, McPhail, Moss, Rochow and Sears families, some of whom are shown below in a 2005 reunion.

While the official opening of the new congregation was set for September 23, 1984[3], the six families held a get-acquainted service of praise and prayer, including a "Sunday School", at the home of the Rochows on September 16, 1984, with approximately twenty-five persons present. This service also included a final planning session for the official opening on the following Sunday.

Beginning on September 23, 1984 until Palm Sunday 1985, the new congregation only met for evening services in the gymnasium of the

Dunning-Foubert Elementary School, while the six families disengaged themselves from their commitments in their churches of origin. During that time, Bert De Roo, the pastor of *Eastview Baptist Church*, Neil Hunter of Bethany and Gunter Rochow led the services one Sunday each per month. On the fourth Sunday, a lay member of the new congregation was in charge, a role which on several occasions fell on Austin Moss. When there were five services in a month, the congregation invited a pastor from another Ottawa area Baptist Church.

During the first fall and winter, the new congregation welcomed many new families who became active participants in this new outreach ministry. They included Darlene Tytula (September 30), Campbell Stephens (October 14), Richard and Helen Turle and their children Karen, Ruth and Paul (October 28) and Betty Stephen (December 23).

In retrospect, the population growth in Orleans far exceeded the fondest expectations of the original church planters. In 1976, the population of Orleans was estimated at 11,000. Ten years later it reached 47,000, and in 2006 the census records reported a population of 95,491!

Support and Steering Committee. To assist the new congregation in its planning, a *Support and Steering Committee* (SSC) was established early in the fall of 1984, which initially functioned under the leadership of the Reverend Neil Hunter [4] and under the general guidance of the Reverend Nelson (Bud) Hooper, then Assistant

Secretary of the BCOQ *Department of Canadian Mission*. In the earliest extant Minutes of the SSC[5], dated June 1985, Richard Turle was identified as the Chairman. The main functions of the SSC were: To develop an organizational structure for the church; appoint officers; call a pastor; and develop a Covenant. On an ongoing basis the duties of the SSC were to perform routine management functions. The specific management functions were: Reporting on BCBC's display at the Convention Assembly; contracting of Heather Voss as organist; making arrangements for a summer Youth Corps; purchasing liability insurance; providing for pulpit supply; undertaking a blitz on September 8 with the participation from other Ottawa Baptist churches; managing the Christian Education program, finances and fellowship events; promoting a Men's Fellowship breakfast; planning the first anniversary service on September 22, as well as future meetings and Sunday School during the summer; and selecting Sunday School materials.[6]

Pastoral Search. The search for a pastor advanced rapidly. Thus, the SSC called a special congregational meeting[7] for January 22, 1985, which was held at the home of Lisee Kiar, to meet the Reverend Don Collar as pastoral candidate. When the congregation assembled its initial criteria for the selection of a pastor, bilingualism in English and French was one of the preferences, due to the fact that Orleans was a bilingual community. However, when Bud Hooper recommended Don Collar, he did so in spite of the fact that Don was unilingual English speaking. Upon meeting Don, it was evident to the congregation that the language issue was not really a significant factor. In presenting himself, Don displayed his characteristic modesty to the point of acknowledging that he lacked experience in church extension and that evangelism was not his special gift; however, he considered his strength to be teaching, exhortation and encouragement.

Don grew up in a Fellowship Baptist Church, was involved with Spring Garden and Highland Baptist Churches, worked in sales and credit related positions, graduated from both the Ontario Bible College and Waterloo University (Conrad Grebel) and was the pastor of St. George Baptist Church from 1979-1985.

In the company of his wife Cathy and his son Bradley, he began his ministry at BCBC on Easter Sunday 1985, and his Induction took place on May 5. [8] Fittingly, the Rev. Bud Hooper delivered the Induction message, and the Rev. Neil Hunter offered the Induction prayer. As part of the Act of Induction, the Minister-Elect and the People exchanged, among others, the following commitments:

Minister-Elect: I will make your needs my service. As a servant of our Lord Jesus Christ, I will seek to use my particular gifts to serve you. Now I ask two things. Will you be sensitive to my personal needs and my limitations, and will you use your talents, as given by God, to assist me in my task as minister?

People: We assure you that we will support you as a person, and that we will apply our particular gifts to the support of the ministry that we now share. We accept you as our Minister.

The Induction was also honoured by the presence of Mayor Peter Clark of Cumberland, the Rev. Tom Sherwood of the Orleans United Church, the Rev. Gordon Kouwenburg of Grace Presbyterian Church and Pastor Brian Eamer of the New Horizon Four Square Gospel Church, who attended among other local ministers.[9]

Constitution. While work began during the first winter of the congregation's existence (1984-1985) to develop elements for the BCBC Constitution, the congregation approved its first version on September 20, 1987, as a part of the third anniversary celebrations. In his 1987 Annual Report of the *Support and Steering Committee*[10], Richard Turle thanked Gunter Rochow, Austin Moss, Don Collar and Ferne Richardson for their work in drafting the Constitution. Amendments were undertaken in January 1993 and in 2005, followed by further amendments that became effective on June 12, 2008 to bring the Constitution into line with the requirements of the Phase II expansion and BCBC's Incorporation in the Province of Ontario.

As of 2008, the Constitution addressed BCBC's understanding of the Church (Article 1), its assets (Article 2), its membership (Article 3), its Board of Directors (Article 4), the Council (Article 5), the Commissions (Article 6), Marriage within the church (Article 7), Church Business Meetings (Article 8), Byelaws (Article 9), Ordinances (Article 10), and Amendments to the Constitution (Article 11).

The Byelaws address: (1) Administrative matters; (2) the Pastoral Ministry; (3) the establishment, membership and functions of the Board of Deacons; (4) the establishment, membership and functions of the Board of Trustees; (5) the appointment, function and term of the office of Treasurer; (6) on the appointment, function and term of the office of Recording Secretary; (7) on the appointment, function and term of the office of Moderator; (8) on the establishment and terms of reference of the Council; (9) the establishment and terms of reference of the Commission of Worship; (10) the establishment and terms of reference of the Commission on Mission; (11) the establishment and terms of reference of the Commission on Evangelism; (12) the establishment and terms of reference of the Commission on Teaching; (13) the establishment and terms of reference of the Commission on

Fellowship; (14) the establishment and terms of reference of the Commission on Service Ministries; (15) the establishment and terms of reference for the use of the Church buildings, facilities, or any other type of asset of the Church.

The Constitution also contains appendices on particular subjects: (A) Marriage Policy, as well as an attachment containing a resolution on Same-Sex Marriage; (B) Covenant of Ethical Pastoral Conduct; (C) Church Policy Statement on Children's Ministry; (D) Bilberry Creek Baptist Church and Église Évangélique Baptiste D'Orléans Covenant; and (E) Articles of Incorporation.

Article 1 of the Constitution identifies the name of the church as *Bilberry Creek Baptist Church*. That name has a political history in that, when the congregation began to meet in 1984 and started to explore potential sites for ultimate construction of a building, nobody knew whether the church would eventually build in the Gloucester, Orleans or Cumberland sectors of Ottawa. In order to avoid a political blunder, Lisee Kiar suggested the name that stuck: *Bilberry Creek*. She made that suggestion because at one time the real *Bilberry Creek* meandered through the Gloucester, Orleans and Cumberland sectors!

Article 3, on membership, represents a mature view of the Church of Jesus Christ, of which Baptists are one expression. The candidates for membership are defined in four categories.

"Any person may be considered as a candidate for membership in Bilberry Creek Baptist Church, provided that person: (3.1.1) is an immersed believer; or, (3.1.2) is a member of another Baptist Church and is able to present a letter of transfer or a commendation from that church; or, (3.1.3) is a member of good standing of another Christian Church, as witnessed in a letter of transfer or commendation, or, if unobtainable, as affirmed by the candidate in a signed letter to Bilberry Creek Baptist Church, which outlines the candidate's past Christian experience, as well as the places and times of that experience; or, (3.1.4) is an individual who has made public confession of faith in Jesus Christ, but who considers baptism inadvisable due to an infirmity or to other extenuating circumstances."

The definition of membership contained in BCBC's Constitution is known as "open membership" in recognition of the fullness of the Body of Christ, as distinct from "associate membership", which limits some rights of members, and "closed membership", which severely restricts many or all rights, in some cases even access to communion, to members of Baptist churches. All three forms of membership are known and practiced in Baptist churches, as discussed in a classic scholarly work by Beasley-Murray.[11] William R. Wood, a respected CBOQ pastor, wrote in a study on communion, baptism and membership in Baptist Churches: "Accompanying open communion, the practice of open membership is acceptable for the benefit of those transferring as professing Christians and church members."[12] BCBC's twenty-five years of experience demonstrate that its definition of membership is not only a good workable option, sanctioned by CBOQ, but that it has produced some of the most faithful and sincere members of its congregation.

Covenant. The Covenant is not a confession of faith, but rather a statement of commitment entered into by members of BCBC and spelling out how they intend to express their Christian faith in practice. The Covenant [13] was first adopted by the 37 charter members on September 20, 1987, i.e. the third anniversary of BCBC's first public service (see Annex D for the order of service for the first public service). It is customary to recite this Covenant publicly whenever new members are being received into the congregation, as well as on Anniversary Sunday. The text of the Covenant is set out in Box 1.

Box 1: Bilberry Creek Baptist Church Covenant

Believing:
- That there is one God
- That God created the universe and sustains it
- That He revealed Himself to us in many ways, supremely through Jesus Christ and through the awareness of His presence as the Holy Spirit, as recorded in the Scriptures
- That through his self-sacrificing love he redeemed man and urges those who respond to him in faith to love one another
- And that the Church is God's chosen instrument to carry out His purpose in the world

Therefore, we as members of Bilberry Creek Baptist Church covenant:
- To worship God
- To strive to know and love Him by searching the Scriptures which are our final authority for faith and practice
- To know and do His will in our daily lives
- To be open to His Fatherly love and to respond to Him in childlike trust
- To share God's love with our fellowmen, by witnessing to our faith through preaching and teaching and through many informal opportunities of our daily life, such as
  - Showing interest and concern in their joys and in their sorrows
  - By caring for them in times of hardship
  - And by helping them to respond to God's love through faith in Jesus Christ
  - To uphold the principles of our distinctive Christian heritage
  - To cooperate with Christians from other traditions in the pursuit of peace and justice in the world and in the anticipation of our Christian hope
  - And to exercise individually, as members of the Body of Christ, our various gifts for service, and to support the ministries of the church at home and abroad, financially and in prayer.

In his final Annual Report (1987) as Chairman of the SSC, Richard Turle pointed out: That henceforth the leadership of the church would pass to elected officials for whom a slate of officers was presented; that the Constitution is being finalized; that recognition by the *Ottawa Baptist Association* (OBA), and, through it, by BCOQ, had been obtained on September 20, 1987, as a precondition for the official founding of the church, which occurred when thirty-seven charter members covenanted on the third anniversary of BCBC's initial public service. In his 1987 Annual Report, Richard also made the point that BCBC must depend for its growth not only on passive population influx into the community but on active evangelistic outreach.

Incorporation. Along with other Baptist Churches, BCBC considered incorporation as early as November 1996.[14] Spring Garden Baptist Church, which had gone that route, provided information from their lawyer to aid other churches in their decisions. Ten years later, in the summer of 2006, and on the advice of its lawyer, Les Bunning, BCBC again considered incorporation before the congregation incurred greater debt. The decision to incorporate led to amendments of the BCBC Constitution, which provides for the establishment of a Board of Directors, consisting of seven elected members: A Chairman who will also be Church Moderator; a member of the Board of Deacons; a member of the Board of Trustees; three members at large; the Treasurer and Recording Secretary as ex-officio members; as well as one member who is unanimously appointed by the other directors, and who is not necessarily a member of BCBC. Among other responsibilities, this Board ensures that the Corporation adheres to all applicable laws and other requirements of the Province of Ontario and of Canada.

Objectives. During its organization process, the Church was careful to stress that it wanted to be perceived as a Baptist Church working cooperatively with, and among, other Christian churches. As stated in the BCBC Constitution, Article 1, it defined its fundamental objective as follows: *"The Church's fundamental objective is to glorify God and to make and nurture disciples."* This basic statement answers to the question "what".

Governance. The governance of the church was assured by several means: Annual meetings, Council, Board of Deacons, Board of Trustees, Commissions, a Treasurer and Recording Secretary, and, since Incorporation in 2008, by a Board of Directors.

Annual Meetings. The Annual Meetings of members of the Church are the formal instruments for reporting and decision making. From the beginning, the Annual Meetings were conducted in two phases: A program planning meeting in June and a budget meeting in late January of the following year. This was done so that the budget would be responsive to program needs.

Council. The BCBC Council was established in April 1988, after the Support and Steering Committee ceased to exist. Council is a decision-making body of the church between annual meetings. Richard Turle was its first Chairman.

Board of Deacons. At BCBC the *Board of Deacons* is responsible for supporting the Pastor in meeting the spiritual needs of the congregation. Their work includes participation in pastoral care and, particularly, in maintaining contact with assigned groups of members and guiding the *Pastoral Care Team*. The latter consists of pastoral care volunteers who have received special training to enable them to identify and respond to spiritual needs. Specific functions[15] of the *Board of Deacons* include the examination and orientation of new members, the semi-annual review with the Pastor of the achievement of planned objectives and goals, advising the Pastor in his ministry and supporting him in the pursuit of his ministry, assisting the Pastor in the conduct of public services, administering disbursements from the benevolent fund, assuring regular pulpit supply, preaching missions and exchanges, and selecting members for participation in serving communion.

Board of Trustees. Under the guidance of Council, the *Board of Trustees* is responsible for the administration of financial and physical assets of the church. In particular, it is responsible[16] for developing financial systems and controls to guide the *Treasurer*, who is an ex-officio member of this Board, the *Envelope Steward* and the *Tellers*. Together with the Treasurer, the Board develops and controls the annual budget. It presents financial reports to the Council and to the congregation and encourages financial stewardship. It sets the terms and conditions of employment, other than the contract with the Pastor. It develops, enters into, and administers, all contractual obligations, including insurance coverage. It acquires and maintains all property and equipment, identifies and supervises ushers, maintains attendance records, and assures appropriate use of church facilities. In that context, the Trustees fulfilled a unique role that was visible to all: the original installation, repair and reinstallation of three memorial crosses, following a severe storm on September 19, 2003.

Commissions. The Church also believed that its objective of *glorifying God and making and nurturing disciples* must be executed in a variety of ways, in accordance with the New Testament teaching. The Church in the New Testament worshipped and glorified God. It preached the Good News and set out to evangelize the world. It taught and nurtured the believers. It rejoiced in fellowship one with the other, and it ministered to the needy in a variety of service ministries. The following diagram visualizes this interrelationship, as originally conceived.

Diagram 1:

The Original Commission Concept

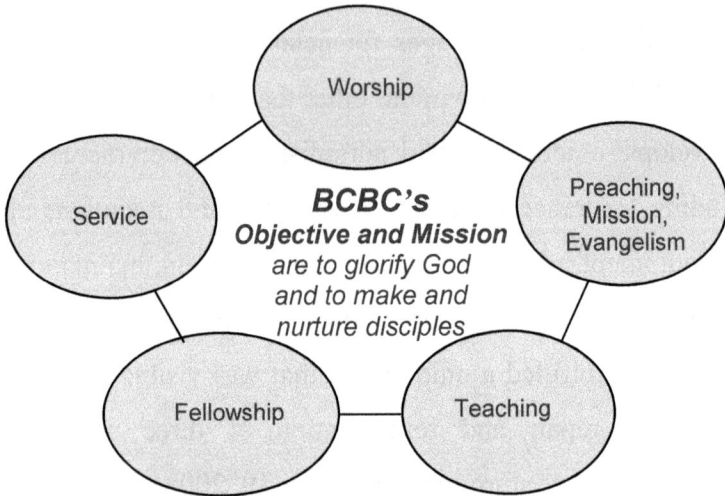

It should be noted that, in naming the Commissions, the Biblical ministry terms were deliberately chosen, rather than secular terms. Thus A "*Teaching*" Commission was envisioned, not an "*Education* Commission", because the New Testament portrayed Jesus as a "teacher" not as an "educator".

During the organization process, when the Church answered the question "how", it believed that a healthy church must combine all these aspects of ministry and act upon them in a unique way to meet the needs of the congregation and community served. Thus, BCBC came to have five initial commissions. How exactly these ministries were carried out could vary over time in response to the unique and changing needs of the congregation. Thus, at a later stage, the *Commission on Preaching, Mission and Evangelism* was renamed to *Mission Commission* and, still later, a new *Commission on Evangelism* was established, with the effect that, at the time of writing, BCBC had six commissions. While these commissions provide a convenient focus for organization and governance, they are nevertheless interrelated and interdependent. The work of the Commissions is discussed in greater detail in Part 2. Over time, other unique groups sprung up in response to need, both within and without the Commission structure.

Board of Directors. In order to comply with the requirements of incorporation in the Province of Ontario, the Church also established a *Board of Directors* in 2008. The first meeting of this Board occurred on June 12, 2008.[17]

Communication. The earliest form of written communication at BCBC was the *Bilberry Creek Baptist Church Challenger*, followed by the establishment of a website and an instant email-based communication tool known as *Bits and Bytes*.

Bilberry Creek Baptist Church Challenger. The Challenger was issued for the first time in October 1988, as *Volume 1, Number 1*. Jim and Pam McPhail won the open contest to name this newsletter, and the congregation approved the proposed name. Gunter Rochow was the first editor and continued in that role until September 1990, when he began a multi-year work program overseas. The associate editors were: Lorraine Donati who reported general news; Austin Moss who drew family sketches of members and adherents; Marguerite Hum who provided Mission news; Patty Lee who designed a page to attract the interest of children; and Barbara Jen who enriched the readers' culinary choices with her articles entitled *My Favorite Recipe*. Chris MacIntyre arranged for word processing.

The contributors to the first edition were: Rev. Don Collar, Lorraine Donati, Ron Waters and Richard Turle jointly, Bob Zelmer, David Oickle, Austin Moss, Marguerite Hum, Barbara Jen and Gunter Rochow.

Don Collar's column, in the first edition, concluded with the words: *As we stand at the present milestone in the life of Bilberry Creek and look back over the path by which God has brought us to this moment, surely we have every reason to exclaim: "When all Thy mercies, O my God, my thankful heart surveys, transported with the view I'm lost, in wonder, love and praise"*. Lorraine Donati provided contact data for the Challenger, a Calendar of Events, times and location for the church service and Sunday School, as well as a welcome column about new members. Ron Waters and Richard Turle described the wide-ranging role of the trustees. Bob Zelmer's column, entitled "The Quest for the Promised Land", described how, on October 30, 1987, the church conveyed two parcels of land on Innes Road to BCOQ as a future building site. David Oickle reported on developments in the Sunday School and on plans for a church library. Austin Moss described his heart transplant on January 15, 1987 and earlier heart surgery in 1980. Appropriately, the title for his column was "A New Beginning – a second chance" (See Box 2). Marguerite Hum introduced the readers to Ron and Marilyn Phillips (CBM: Brazil), referred to completion of the New Testament for the Piaroa Tribe (Venezuela), and sought prayer for the Macu Indians of Colombia, who came out of the jungle in search of missionaries to help them. Barbara Jen provided a recipe for her Apple Pumpkin Coffee Cake. Patty Lee had a fun activity page for children. Gunter Rochow offered an Editorial, as well as a photo of the pioneers, a "study nugget" on the origin of the word "paradise", as well as a Bible question.

Box 2. Austin Moss: A New Beginning – a second chance

Austin referenced Ezekiel 36: 26 and 27. Then he added: "On June 9, 1987 I was watching a Billy Graham telecast and Mr. Graham pointed his finger to the people and the TV camera and asked, 'Won't you give your heart today to Jesus?' Well, I said, hey Billy I have a New Heart that I want to dedicate to the Lord. The next Sunday I dedicated my New Heart to the Lord.

Praise be to God for this NEW BEGINNING".

Patty Lee was the editor of the Challenger from December 1990 until December 1991, followed by Bonny Miskowicz , who served as editor from October 1992 until October 1994. Jean Normand was the longest serving editor, from April 1995 until Easter 2003. In her last issue she worked together with Jeff Parke; however shortly thereafter the Parkes moved away from the Orleans area, which necessitated the intervention of an interim editor, whose name could not be ascertained. Beginning with the April 2004 issue, Crystal and Martin Thieringer took over the editorship, followed by Jen Messer, and a special issue for BCBC's 25th Anniversary, which was prepared by Gail Lyons.

Over the years, under the leadership of various editors, the size, contents and presentational format of the Challenger have changed. Beginning in April 1995, the use of the traditional numbering system fell into disuse. The most recent innovation occurred in April 2004, when Crystal and Martin Thieringer gave the lowly traditional Challenger a new professional look, which Jennifer Messer, the subsequent editor, has maintained.

Website. Over time, Dawn McCleave, Waldo Rochow, Jennifer Messer, Don Collar and Brad Collar have contributed to the development of the website and have served as webmaster. The website had several purposes, which were to provide basic information about the church, its programs and special events, as well as to publish the Pastor's weekly sermon notes. The church received responses to the website from far beyond the Orleans community. One reader wrote from France. A grandmother from Boston, MA, saw the BCBC website and called Pastor Collar to ask for the congregation's prayers for Willy, her grandson who was having open heart surgery.[18]

Bits and Bytes. Under the leadership of Gail Lyons, this email-based communication with the congregation shared items of praise, prayer requests and announcements, as they occurred.

Chapter 2: Reaching out to the French-speaking Community

While the BCBC congregation had initially hoped to find a bilingual pastor, God had His own way to meet the needs of the community for both an English and French speaking ministry.

On Sunday evening, September 17, 1989, in collaboration with the Rev. Robert Godin,[19] then Pastor of *Église Baptiste d'Ottawa*, BCBC offered Sunday evening studies in French at the *Bilberry Baptist Centre* on Innes Road. However, these were discontinued after eight weeks when, despite advertising in the community, no French speakers could be attracted. The congregation concluded regretfully that the right time might not yet have come.[20] Nevertheless, Pastor Godin resumed evangelizing in Orleans during the following year, and the interest by both churches in reaching out to the French speaking part of the community continued.

About eight years later, the Rev. Frankie Narcisse,[21] then the Pastor of the *Église Baptiste Évangélique d'Ottawa* initiated a prayer ministry in 1995 in anticipation of an outreach to the Francophone community beginning the following year. An evening service was held in Orleans on March 2, 1997 under the leadership of Pastor Frankie Narcisse and a group of missioners from *Église Baptiste Évangélique d'Ottawa*.[22] On a continuing basis, the first service as *Église Évangélique Baptiste d'Orléans* (EE) was held in the BCBC facilities on January 3, 1999, with attendance ranging between 20 and 50. The community was alerted to this ministry by means of a bilingual brochure distributed in Orleans through the Ad-Bag service. To support the ministry, EE hired summer students to conduct youth and children's outreach".

The "right time" seemed to have come, when, unbeknownst to each other, and on the same day, both BCBC and *Église Baptiste d'Ottawa* were simultaneously in prayer about establishing a French speaking ministry. A discussion document and recommendations from the BCBC Phase II Committee described the next steps, as follows:

> "A steering committee was established, and Pastor George Wagner was called to be the pastor of the fledgling congregation. Under his leadership the congregation was officially received into the Ottawa Association of Baptist Churches and accepted into membership of the BCOQ in the spring of 2000. *Église Évangélique Baptiste d'Orléans* (EE) is the first congregation having dual status. They will be official members of both the French Union and BCOQ.

> With a core of 20 members, EE is energetically reaching out to the francophone community. They have regular Sunday afternoon Bible classes at 2:45 and worship at 3:30. Prayer and outreach have been their focus throughout the early stages of

their ministry. God has blessed their efforts by drawing an average of 50 people to their Sunday gatherings.

A spirit of cooperation continues to exist between our two congregations. As Pastor Collar, Pastor Wagner and Pastor Narcisse meet each month for prayer and encouragement, they celebrate what God has done and continues to do through their people.

It is evident that while each congregation has very distinctive ministries, there is much that can be, and is being, done in partnership to reach Orleans with the gospel.[23]

When *Église Évangélique Baptiste d'Orléans* was launched in January 1998,[24] it was co-located in the same building with BCBC. However, as a result of BCBC's Phase II expansion in 2009, the relationship between the two congregations became one of "Partnership among Equals", formalized in the BCBC Constitution.[25]

While each congregation develops its own program, both frequently engage jointly in certain special events. Thus, at the occasion of Pastor George Wagner's ordination on April 26, 2003, several BCBC members participated in the event, and the Rev. Don Collar pronounced the closing prayer.

Other cooperative events included Anniversary services, Christmas services and Petrie Island outreach activities on Canada Day. A unique feature during joint functions is the presentation of special music by an integrated choir from both congregations. EE and BCBC collaborated in the HOPE 2000 Evangelistic Campaign.

Although CBOQ had provided a $25,000 grant for work at BCBC in the French language in 1997, difficulties arose in 2002, when the *Union of French Baptist Churches* withdrew its support from the EE and CBOQ was unable to provide further help. While BCBC initially provided space to the French congregation on a lease basis, which could be forgiven, the French congregation contributed one third of the insurance premium, made some cash donations, and in 2002 bought and installed a carpet.

From left to right: Pasteur Jérémie Saintilma, Pasteur Franky Narcisse, Pasteur George Wagner, and Pastor Don Collar.

Chapter 3: From Rented Facilities to Our Own Space

BCBC's physical accommodation can be conveniently grouped into two main periods: First, the transitional accommodation before the acquisition of the Charlemagne site, and second, the development of the Charlemagne site in two phases. The transitional accommodation consisted of rented space in two schools as well as, in October 1987, the purchase of two adjacent Innes Road properties.[26] As for the schools, the *Dunning-Foubert Elementary School*[27] served the newly established congregation on Sunday evenings during the first fall and winter. The move to *Our Lady of Wisdom Catholic School*[28] coincided with the arrival of Don Collar as full-time pastor and the initiation of Sunday morning services on Easter Sunday 1985. The physical setting in the library of this school was a big improvement in itself over the rather sterile environment of the gymnasium of the Dunning-Foubert School, even though that school had served the congregation very well. Moreover, Our Lady of Wisdom School permitted the use of classrooms for the Sunday School.

The acquisition of two adjoining Innis Road properties, of which BCBC took possession in 1988, Côté House on April 1 and Allard House in June, represented the Church's first foothold in the real estate market,[29] which later facilitated the property swap under which BCBC was able to obtain its current Charlemagne site. Côté House, which was later renamed *Bilberry Baptist Centre*, formally opened on Covenant Sunday, September 1989, with ribbon cutting by Dr. Keith Cooney.[30] While this facility was never used for Sunday worship, since it was too small, it served well for Sunday Evening Bible studies, Mid-week Ladies' Community Bible Studies, Friday Night Pre-Teen events, adult fellowship meetings, as well as Commission and Council meetings.

Initially a *Site Committee* had been established, which in January 1990 became the *Building Committee*, which was chaired by Bob Zelmer, and whose members were Robert Allsopp and Daryl Grierson.[31]

Initially, in April 1988 a Five-Year Plan was developed, which in October 1988 resulted in a Joint Development Agreement with *Madigan Development* for the Innes Road Site;[32] however, this agreement collapsed in January 1989. Subsequently, Henry Donati, of the BCBC congregation, worked very hard to clarify the church's land development options, shooting photos from a Cessna aircraft, formulating agreements with BCBC's neighbours and negotiating with developers in Montreal and Toronto. As a result, on July 20, 1989, a firm deal under favourable terms was reached with *Coscan Development Corporation* to exchange the Côté and Allard properties for a site on Charlemagne Blvd.[33]

Box 3. In Expectation of the Next Miracle

Excerpt from an article written by Bob Zelmer in June 1991 in anticipation of our proceeding with Phase I. It still speaks to us during the construction of Phase II.

... We have been touched by miracles already. Those of us involved with the site committee saw some of these face to face! How else could we have assembled the initial site on Innes Road, when professional land developers had tried to do the same and failed? How else could we have obtained the Bilberry Baptist Centre rent-free for years and with property improvements? How else could we have received the Charlemagne site pre-zoned and pre-serviced at no additional cost at all? Trust me, it was not by our own negotiation skills!

And we have all seen amazing things as we grow week by week at Bilberry. Sometimes these miracles are the people themselves, who come with talents to work with us, the teachers, the musical ones, the well-studied, the caring, the hospitable, the listeners, and the givers. Sometimes it is those among us who struggle and overcome, and by doing so, show us the fruit of our hope and our prayers. Sometimes the miracle is the one we have awaited, or not even expected. We are not strangers to such as these.

The development of the Charlemagne site occurred in two phases: Phase I between April and October 1993, and Phase II, beginning in

2009 and continuing into 2010. In preparation for Phase I, BCOQ transferred the land on Charlemagne Boulevard to BCBC, and BCBC relinquished the lease on the *Bilberry Baptist Centre*. When planning for Phase I began, the church was guided by three fundamental questions that also applied to planning for Phase II: How big will we grow? What programs will we offer? What will we be able to pay for?[34] Architect Harry Ala-Kantti,[35] who was responsible for the design of many important buildings in the Ottawa area, designed the Phase I structure with utility and economy in mind: A single fellowship hall, with kitchen, washroom facilities and foyer, coupled with six integrated, but "plug-in, plug-out" portable modules to provide space for the Pastor's office, Sunday School, counselling, group meetings, as well

as, on a rental basis, midweek space for the private music school *Music Alive*. The architect avoided building a basement, which is often cost-inefficient, but he provided for a unique feature, connecting the congregation with the Creator, by using

several patio doors on two sides that permitted the worshipper to look out into nature. This feature also proved to be a tool for evangelism in that curious outsiders were able to look in, and at least one of these,

Scott Angel, became a member of the congregation. The Dedication Service for the new building occurred on June 5, 1994, [36] just under ten years after BCBC's ministry began!

For years after the building had been completed, the Architect commented to all who would listen that this was in large measure a cooperative undertaking by the members and adherents

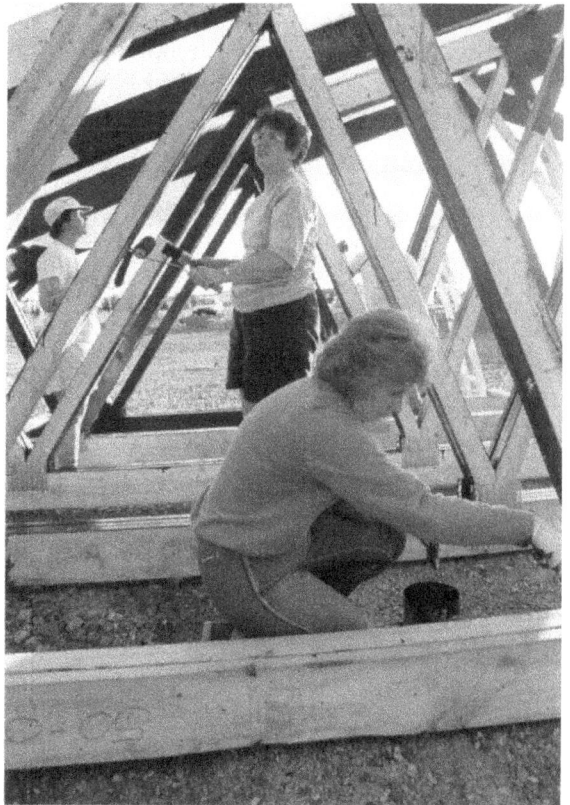

of the church. By way of example, he explained that children were involved in painting as high as they could reach; then adults took over, up into the rafters! Church volunteers helped to build the deck. From outside the congregation, Canadian Baptist Volunteers came to help build two modules, it being understood that these would ultimately be returned to the Ottawa Baptist Association for use in other new churches.[37] Fittingly, the Building Committee suggested the wording of the cornerstone plaque as *Partners Together With Christ*.

While most of the names of volunteers[38] are unknown, since these had not been recorded, and since most probably did not expect that such a record would be kept, some names are known. For instance, Winston Caesar and Gilbert Côté waxed the floor. Russ Delaney and Gilbert Côté donated the chairs. The banners *Peace*, *Hope*, *Love* and *Joy* were prepared by Sharon Basque with help from Claire Rendall and Helen Turle. Daryl Grierson and Bob Zelmer built the cross for the sanctuary and Donna Zelmer made the *I Am* banner, reflecting Easter. This was a cooperative effort, involving Bob Zelmer, Daryl Grierson and Jack Shearer, and Builders' Warehouse loaned their crane. As a Christmas gift to the church, Don and Cathy Collar bought the platforms from Eaton's when the store closed. The stage from Eaton's and the sound system were all wired by Robert Allsop, Bing Hum, and later, as needed, by Barry Francis and Don Vinette.

When the *Uplands' Elizabeth Park Protestant Chapel* was being closed, Major Gary Tonks, who was the chaplain on the base, acquired some of the pews, two deacons' benches and the pulpit.[39] After hours of work, Gary rebuilt the pulpit and made the deacons benches that are currently in use. Since not everything could be provided at once, the congregation rented, as a makeshift baptistry, a whirlpool bath from "Wet and Wild Spas" and set it up on the rear deck. Later Bob Foster donated a formal baptismal unit in memory of his mother. The main room of the fellowship hall was named *Campbell Hall*[40] in memory of Jean Campbell, formerly of First Baptist Church, Perth, in view of the substantial support which that church had

Orléans Community Weekly Journal

PHOTO BY STAN RADFORD

RAISING THE CROSS

Parishioners of Bilberry Creek Baptist Church in Fallingbrook recently volunteered their time raise three memorial crosses to remember deceased loved ones. (Above) Rev. Don Collar secures a support while parishioners Daryl Grierson and Jack Shearer build a rock base. Builders Warehouse volunteered the use of a crane to help the church with the project. Please see the Goodwill Ambassador on page 8 for details.

provided to BCBC's Phase I initiative. A special event was the dedication of the memorial crosses on Anniversary Sunday 1996.[41]

While construction of Phase I was still in progress, Richard Turle recommended in his Trustee Report,[42] that the Building Committee that had guided Phase I planning and construction be reorganized at the end of 1993 to give thought to Phase II. In actual fact the Phase II Building Committee was established in 2000 during the Annual Program Meeting[43]. Nevertheless, that foresight was remarkable and indicates the degree of continuity of thinking between the two phases.

Box 4. Greetings from the Poussett's.
May 28, 1994
To our friends at Bilberry Creek:

Congratulations on the dedication of your new church facility! Several things came to mind on this special day – the many long hours that you dedicated to this project, the cooperation and support of so many individuals and churches in the Ottawa area, and, most importantly, the way in which God provided so many miracles over the past year, in locating and building the church in its present location.

We are happy to have been part of the fellowship at Bilberry for three years. We remember our time in the Ottawa area with a great deal of fondness, and often think of you all. Although we were not able to see the building project through to its completion, we are happy to have served with you throughout the planning and design stages. (Please send us a picture; we have yet to see the completed building!)

We know that this building had long been a dream for many of you. Now that it is a reality, we pray that it may be used as a stepping stone for further outreach into the Orleans community. Love, in Christ,

Dan, Lorraine, Stephen, Jordan, & Kaleigh Poussett

One of the first steps of the new Phase II Building Committee was to survey[44] the membership, this to be completed by June 10, 2001, with a view to identifying the congregation's expected needs and wishes. However, more than two years later, in December 2003, the Phase II Building Committee still wanted to hear "dreams", and from November 12-14, 2004 BCBC held a "Futuring Workshop", [45] facilitated by the Rev. Jeff Hill, to crystallize the congregation's vision. Basing itself on the survey results, the "dreams" and the vision, the planning for Phase II was a complex process in that it involved both the BCBC and EE congregations and the desire to ensure that the mortgage for Phase I was completely paid before Phase II financial commitments were assumed. On the advice of BCBC's lawyer, Les Bunning, the church also proceeded with incorporation before assuming new debt. In particular, much time was devoted to defining the modalities of collaboration between the two congregations that would use the facility, with special effort made to ensure that both BCBC and EE would be able to have their worship services on Sunday mornings.

In both Phase I and Phase II there were clear expectations for the desired maximum size of the congregation. In the case of Phase I, there was sufficient accommodation for 200 people; in the case of Phase II, the new building will accommodate 400[46] people at one time. This means that a total of 600 people can worship simultaneously, using the two units. The rationale for limiting physical space in the new building to 400 is that a larger congregation would likely lead to less participatory effort by the members, and thus fewer opportunities for ministry, and that from an evangelistic perspective it would be more desirable to encourage outreach into new areas once the planned maximum is reached.

In particular, the Phase II activity required many steps and countless hours of volunteers, under the leadership of the Phase II Building Committee[47], which was chaired by Richard Turle. The outline sketch, or footprint, for the entire project, which had been produced by the Architect Ralph Vandenberg, had to be finalized. To do so, the initial sketch was used to consult all Commissions and other users of the space to confirm the adequacy of the sketch. On September 10, 2008 the agreed upon draft plans were taken to the City of Ottawa for pre-site plan approval. That meeting was attended by Richard Turle, Ralph Vandenberg and the Construction Manager Richard Bossman of *BBS Construction*. Since it was obvious that not all Phase II plans could be executed at once, the plan was divided into two sub-phases: Phase IIA and Phase IIB. Nevertheless, to accomplish Phase IIA, the details of Phase IIB were required. The goals of Phase IIA were to provide initially 400 seats in order also to accommodate meeting and classroom space, as well as additional washrooms and a new larger foyer. In Phase IIB it is expected that all modules may be moved in accordance with then prevailing needs. The actual capacity at the time of completion of Phase IIA was 390 seats.

Following the September 10, 2008 meeting with the City, which went very well, the application for a site plan expansion were posted later in the fall and the neighbours were notified. The detailed design phase and the identification of potential subcontractors, as well as a formal application to the City for a building permit followed. Final congregational approval coincided with the annual budget meeting in February 2009.

The Groundbreaking ceremony occurred on April 26, 2009[48]. Actual construction started marginally later than planned due to delays by the City of Ottawa in issuing certain required documents.

Nevertheless, planning for the usage of space proceeded simultaneously, a formidable task that had been assigned to Bradley Collar (BCBC) and Deholo Nali (EE). During the construction process space was at a premium, at one point without access to a single module! At that time the foyer was used for Junior Church and the Nursery, and the Music School *Music Alive*[49] had been relocated temporarily to the home of Janice and Douglas Rochow. In expectation of things to come, no murmurs were heard.

Chapter 4: Church Finance

The overall responsibility for the administration of financial and physical assets of the Church rests with the Board of Trustees. In particular, the Trustees are responsible for developing financial systems and controls to guide the Treasurer.

Joyful stewardship by members and adherents is the cornerstone of BCBC's finance. That includes both giving and careful spending. At all times, expectations were balanced against what the Church could afford. The Church used a two-tier budgeting system to distinguish between essential basic and additional discretionary spending, the latter to be activated if funds were available. To encourage regular giving, especially when people are absent for extended periods, the opportunity for making pre-authorized remittances (PAR) [50] was started in the spring of 2004. To reduce the cost of expenditures for the church, each expenditure item is being examined carefully. In the case of insurance,[51] the Trustees renegotiated insurance coverage in 2002-2003 at a considerably reduced annual premium, of which EE paid one third. Publicly available sources of finance were explored to help pay for one or more summer youth workers, such as *Ontario Works* grants, or similar grants available from *Human Resources and Social Development Canada* (HRSDC).[52]

Since the beginning of church construction, financing was a collective effort of the congregation together with BCOQ and individual Baptist churches. The Phase I funding sources were: (1) The Division of Shared Mission of BCOQ ($100,000); (2) First Baptist Church, Perth, which provided a $50,000 interest free loan for seven years; and (3) a line of credit from the Bank of Montreal, guaranteed by BCOQ, up to $350,000, for a maximum of $450,000. The Phase II approved borrowing was up to $1,550,000, of which $750,000 came from BCOQ and $800,000 from The Bank of Nova Scotia.

During Phase I, and apart from the above mentioned major blocks of funding, BCBC benefitted from other forms of financing, including grants and gifts. The *Ottawa Association of Baptist Churches* raised $65,000 for the five modules, on the understanding that the modules would remain Association property and could be reassigned elsewhere, when needed. *Fourth Avenue Baptist Church* provided collateral to secure a line of credit for BCBC, initially at $25,000, and then lowered to $10,000 to cover emergencies. In addition to its $50,000 loan, First Baptist Church, Perth, provided a donation of $4,800, and Olivet Baptist Church, Sarnia, donated $5,000. Cornwall First Baptist Sunday School provided financial assistance of $750.00 for BCBC's Sunday School. BCOQ provided a $25,000 grant for French work at BCBC, i.e. for *Église Évangélique Baptiste d'Orléans*.[53]

Within BCBC, church finance consisted of regular and special Sunday offerings, memorial contributions, rent for use of space by *Music Alive* and by *Lifeline Counselling*, contributions in lieu of rent and in-kind contributions, e.g. carpeting, by *Église Évangélique Baptiste d'Orléans,* as well as fundraising for such expenditures as the paving of the parking lot, a heater, platforms and speakers, for which the women raised $1,683 and the youth $1,200 in a particular year. Baking apple pies was a social event led by Elaine Eckert, which in 2001 alone raised $600 as a contribution towards a new dishwasher, a practice that continued on an annual basis. Thus the total cost of the dishwasher of about $3,000 was eventually largely covered by contributions from fellowship events.

To help assess readiness for Phase II, BCBC contracted *Harder and Associates* of Peterborough to lead a stewardship and Phase II fundraising initiative. [54] In 2006, EE contributed $5,000 for the screening process for the selection of an architect and in 2008 it paid for a Sound Booth.

BCBC was not only a recipient of financial assistance from other churches, but it, in turn, contributed. Thus, in 2003, BCBC contributed to the new Longfields Baptist Church $1,500 through the 2003 budget, plus $1,400 in the form of a special collection from a Musical Evening on March 2, 2003; a second gift of $2,000 was sent to Longfields for the purchase of land. Small occasional grants were also made to such organizations as the *Miriam Centre*.

BCBC also endeavored to pay regular BCOQ per member contributions of $100 per member and *Ottawa Baptist Association* dues. However, in practice some of those payments were offset by other contributions. For instance, in 2003, when BCBC had 108 members, it would have owed BCOQ $10,800. However, that year BCBC assumed the EE rental component, which was valued at $14,400 and made $3,500 in contributions to Longfields, for a total of $17,900. On the other hand, BCBC decided to pay the Ottawa Association dues for 2004 in 2003 in order to take advantage of the lower 2003 rates. In the area of salaries, BCBC increased the Pastor's salary by a discretionary amount of $1,500 in recognition of additional activities, such as mentoring other pastors at the request of BCOQ.

PART II: THE MINISTRY

BILBERRY – *A Seed in Good Soil*

Chapter 5: Pastoral Ministry and Support

As pastor-elect, Don Collar made the following commitment to the church: I will make your needs my service. As a servant of our Lord Jesus Christ, I will seek to use my particular gifts to serve you. Now I ask two things. Will you be sensitive to my personal needs and my limitations, and will you use your talents, as given by God, to assist me in my task as minister? In turn, the congregation responded: We assure you that we will support you as a person, and that we will apply our particular gifts to the support of the ministry that we now share. We accept you as our Minister.

In retrospect, twenty-five years later, there is no doubt in anyone's mind that Don was God's special gift to this congregation, for many reasons. He used a co-operative model of ministry. He fostered acceptance and inclusion, which attracted Christians from various ethnic and church backgrounds. He was a consensus builder. He practiced servant leadership, leading by example and positive spiritual influence. In turn, the congregation allowed him to be himself, including the enjoyment of his motorcycle!

As a pastor, Don performed all expected pastoral duties, preaching on Sundays, participating in teaching Sunday School, when needed, and leading some midweek Bible Studies, caring for the congregation's spiritual and emotional needs and for those of others outside, baptizing new believers, uniting couples in marriage, burying the dead and comforting those close to them. He was a pastor. A Catholic visitor and his United Church girl friend at a recent wedding commented to the authors of this history that when they get married they want to be married in a Baptist Church, because the pastor's meditation was so practical and so near to real life. That says it all. One of the highlights in Don's preaching ministry was an invitation to BCBC from the Canadian Broadcasting Corporation to host the first televised service on September 22, 1996 in their 1996-1997 series "Meeting Place: Canadians at Worship".[55]

Don was not only BCBC's pastor. He was also Military Chaplain of the 28 Service Battalion and Canadian Forces Primary Reserve Chaplain, Brigade Chaplain for 33 Combat Brigade Group, which included the difficult task of coordinating next-of-kin notifications for fallen soldiers. As Brigade Chaplain he supervised Reserve Chaplains in Northern and Eastern Ontario. In these roles, Don has risen to the military rank of Major. Don also served as Chaplain of the Orleans Branch 623 of the Royal Canadian Legion, which allowed him to provide pastoral care to members without church connection and to assist with "Operation Recuperation" during "Ice Storm '98". On a short-term basis he served as On-Call Chaplain at Base Uplands while their Padre was in Golan Heights. Commenting on these roles, Don noted that the majority of the Militia have never been involved in church or heard the Gospel. His dual role as pastor and chaplain had a very beneficial impact for BCBC, in that Don was constantly involved in ministering to people from many Christian backgrounds, which fostered understanding, sensitivity and acceptance.

As an aspect of his broader ministry, Don also visited the Ottawa Detention Centre when he knew an inmate at a family's request. By request of BCOQ/CBOQ, Don mentored several new pastors, who included Bruce McCallum from Breadalbane Baptist Church, and Tom Smith (2002-2003), Jim Perking and Wayne Sollows (2003-2004), Mr. Gerald Claybourne, of Maple Avenue Baptist Church, Brownsburg, Québec.

Box 5. A Story of Answered Prayers
Submitted by Jun Zhang (BCBC Challenger, Dec. 2007, p. 6). Note: Jun Zhang is herself a medical doctor.

Joey has had eczema since he was born. The illness exacerbated when Joey was about 7-8 years old. Eczema is an allergic condition that

---

affects the skin. For some people, eczema is a life-time struggle to control the itchy, red, weeping and painful condition of the skin.

When Joey was in Grade 3, his skin condition was getting worse and worse every day. With the disease progressing rapidly, approximately 90%-95% of Joey's skin was covered by rash and scratches, and over 50% of the skin had turned brownish, scaly and had thickened. The itching was so intense that it often interfered with his sleep and other daytime activities. He even tried not to be with other kids because he did not want them to see his skin.

We tried almost every possible way to treat his eczema. We tried prescription medications, including the most recently approved drugs. They did not work. We tried Chinese herb medicines; they did not work well either. We tried to avoid triggering factors, change eating habits; nothing really worked. A dermatologist examined Joey and concluded that Joey would carry the illness for the rest of his life since he had the most severe form of eczema she had ever seen. Hearing this conclusion, Joey was crying and my heart was crying too. I cried out to the Lord from my heart, "Lord, please have mercy on Joey and help him".

As we were losing our hope, one Sunday service the church was carrying out a prayer section for healing. Pastor Don asked people who needed prayers to come to the front. I took Joey's hands and together we walked up. Pastor pointed oil on Joey's fore-head and prayed for him. Immediately, I felt something and a peace came into my heart as we were walking back to our seats. I knew that we can trust the Lord for He loves and cares for Joey.

After the special prayers on that beautiful Sunday morning, Joey's skin started getting better and better without using any prescription or Chinese herb medicines. The thickened skin started to become normal; the rashes started to disappear; the itching became less intense. Remarkably Joey's eczema disappeared.

It has been about three years since the prayers. Joey's skin remains in a normal condition. Currently, there is no rash or itching. Joey is in Grade 10 and is doing well in school. He has many friends and is involved in many activities.

I am thankful for the prayers of Pastor Don and other members of the congregation. I believe this is God's miracle and I am very thankful for what the Lord has done for Joey and for our family.

In terms of inter-church and inter-faith relations, Don served as Secretary-Treasurer and as Chairperson of the Greater Orleans Ministerial Association, later renamed as East Ottawa Christian Ministerial Association, and maintained informal contacts with a varying number of other pastors over time. Pastors who participated came from the following churches: Anglican, Baptist (Fellowship and BCBC), Brethren, Four-Square, Independent (Église de la Nouvelle Alliance), Lutheran, Pentecostal, Presbyterian, Roman Catholic (English) and United.[56] In Don's experience, these relationships, while important to him, were not always reciprocated, since not all pastors shared the same sense of importance of fellowshipping with pastors of backgrounds other than their own. This is one area where Don would very much have liked to see improvement. Nevertheless, Don was encouraged to have been invited in 1989 by Our Lady of Wisdom Catholic School to participate, along with the Rev. Gordon Kouwenberg (Grace Presbyterian Church) and Father Delaney (Divine Infant Catholic Church) in a service of Christian Unity. For many years, Don received similar invitations from the school to speak to the children about Christian unity. This stopped when a new Principal had been appointed at that school.

On a monthly basis, Don met with a group called "Jewish/Christian Dialogue". This forum provided an excellent opportunity for Christians and Jews to learn from, and to appreciate, each other. In the context of appreciation of our Judeo-Christian heritage, BCBC conducted a Seder supper as early as 1998. In the Jewish tradition, the Seder is a ritual at which the story of the liberation of the Israelites from slavery in ancient Egypt is retold.

With respect to the Muslim community, the Presbyterian Record published the following note on "Ministers building bridges in the wake of September 11":

> Some ministers in Ottawa's east end have put their concerns about racial violence arising from the September 11 terrorist attack into action. Don Collar of Bilberry Baptist Church, Dennis Gruver of New Wine Community Church and Jim Statham of Grace Presbyterian Church in Orleans, along with Christian businessman Gunter Rochow and Abdul Rashid, a leader of Ottawa's Muslim Community have offered to speak to Orleans high schools on "Building Bridges in the Community after September 11." The action was prompted by a desire to foster tolerance and understanding in the community

in the wake of the vicious beating of a local Muslim youth on September 15. At the group's initial meeting in mid-September, the discussion ranged from identifying the roots of violence to what Christians can do to help curb this kind of prejudice and hostility." [57]

While there was no take-up of this offer in the Public Schools, it is evident that the Christians were indeed building bridges to the Muslim community, as BCBC did with its refugee sponsorship of Mohamud Issa, a young Muslim from Somalia, which is discussed below.

Rev. Tom Sherwood, chaplain of Carleton University at the time and Rabbi Reuven Bulka of the Congregation Machzikei Hadas [58] first began the monthly dialogues. Dr. Sam Raj, of Orleans Centre for Marriage and Family was another participant from Orleans. Sam invited Don Collar to attend the informal gatherings over lunch. These gatherings were informative as participants talked about faith, peace and justice and other related issues. This dialogue was not started by any particular ministerial.

In 2003-2004 Don served as one of the hosts of the program *All Praise Him*, on CHRI, Ottawa's Christian Radio Station. For 2004-2005, Don sat on the Board of Directors for "Daily Adventures Ministries", which Kevin Bloodworth's vision for children and youth ministry in Canada was sponsoring.

At the community level, Don performed an enormous number of functions for which he was honoured by receiving the Queen's Jubilee Medal. Don's community work included: The supervision of persons required to do community service under Community Service Orders (CSO); membership on the Board of Directors of Cumberland Senior Citizens Village, and Chairman of the Board of the Gloucester Emergency Food Cupboard. In this latter role, it is noteworthy that this service, which was provided by two part-time staff and 100 volunteers, reaches over 20,000 people annually, half of whom are children.

In view of his multiple roles, Don sought many opportunities to fine-tune his already impressive skills, by registering in a Masters Program in Pastoral Care at St. Paul's University, by studying "Theories of Counseling" with Dr. Paul O'Grady, by participating in a Church Planting Conference, organized by the CBOQ's Department of Shared Missions; and by participating in short-courses such as the following: "Drug and Alcohol Educator's Course" (Kingston); "Peacekeeping and humanitarian operations course" (Camp Borden); "Contemporary Music in the Church"; "Spiritual Warfare"; "Small Groups"; "Conflict Resolution"; and in 2003-2004 the "Suicide Intervention Program".

As tools for ministry, Don published a number of statements in BCBC's website[59], which are also available in paper upon request. They include: Marriage and the Family; Divorce; Suicide; Care for the

Dying; Sanctity of Human Life; and Homosexuality. Don's weekly sermons are also published on BCBC's website.

Youth Leaders. Volunteers served as Youth Leaders virtually from the start, except for 1989-1990 when Don Collar assumed that role: Robyn and David Oickle (1984-1986), Fred and Rene Weiss (1986-1988), Mary Wehrle and Helen Turle (1991-1994), and Ruth Turle (1994-1999).

Minister of Youth. Since 2002, BCBC benefitted from an expanded pastoral team, with Jillian Zelmer serving as Minister of Youth beginning on September 30, 2002. She brought several strong qualifications to the task, including a B.A. (Hons.) in psychology, as well as work experience with the Mission Commission, Christian camps and Inter-Varsity Christian Fellowship (IVCF), which included serving as President of the Carleton University IVCF Chapter, as well as participating in an IVCF mission trip to Ecuador.[60] Shortly after her appointment, Don Collar met with her to discuss measurable performance expectations, indicating that both of them would meet regularly to review these.

One of Jillian's first activities was to set up an executive committee of three to four youths, which functioned in conjunction with an adult support group. Ensuring the continuing delivery of earlier youth related activities now became one of her oversight responsibilities. Thus, the first Pre-Teen group meeting under her leadership occurred on October 4, 2002. Other early youth work involved BCBC participation in "Acquire the Fire" at the Corel Centre.[61]

In her first Annual Report [62], Jillian identified the following organizational structure for her youth work, comprising: (1) the GAP (God Answers Prayer) Youth Group (high school or 13 years and older youths); (2) a Junior High Group (grades 7-8 or ages 11 and 12); and (3) Pre-teens (grades 5-6, or ages 9 and 10). Jeff Parke served as the adult volunteer for the GAP Group, Helen Meubus for the Junior High group and Robert Allsopp for Pre-Teens, with the help of Andrea Rochow.

Apart from organization, the reported highlights of GAP for the first year included: Training seminars, city-wide events, including worship and prayer, fund-raising activities such as raking leaves and a pancake supper in support of local and out-of-town youth events, a Youth Worship Service with Drama in November and a morning worship service in May, a 30 hour famine which raised $500 for World Vision, as well as social events such as bowling, movies and sleep-overs. It is noteworthy that by 2008-2009, the annual 30 hour famine raised $1,896.00 in this effort![63]

Junior High activities usually included discussion time, games and snacks, as well as Bible studies from a book called *Faith Metaphors*, which contains many interactive object lessons.

Programming for Pre-Teens usually included discussion time, games from *Ultimate Book of Preteen Games* and snacks, as well as Bible studies from *Faith Metaphors.* During the year, two meetings for parents of the youth groups were held (with disappointing attendance) to hear how parents think the youth have been impacted. Jillian attended all *Exousia* meetings of Ottawa Youth Workers, which were held monthly at St. Paul's Presbyterian Church under the leadership of Paul Racine of Dulos Ministries for sharing and supporting each other in prayer. On occasion, Pre-teens and Junior Highs participated in joint activities, such as a wave swim and an indoor glow-in-the-dark mini-putt.

Programming for subsequent years was similar. Nevertheless, in 2003-2004, a GAP special event was a March break mission trip to Montreal. Jillian also assisted Don Collar in conducting the baptismal classes.[64] In 2006, Sunday Night Live (meal, worship and discussion) was introduced for young adults and high school students.[65]

When Jillian resigned from her role on January 31, 2008, Don Collar, as Senior Pastor, expressed his and the congregation's sadness over Jillian's resignation "as our Minister of Youth after 5 years of excellent ministry"[66]. Following her resignation, Brett Brule, Luke Cavey, Colin Dickinson and Mark Bunning led the youth work on an interim basis.[67]

Pastor to Youth and Young Families. Following Jillian's resignation, Bob Dickenson chaired a search committee that, on May 25, 2008 resulted in the congregation extending a unanimous call to the Rev. Dean Noakes, which he accepted, to become Pastor to Youth and Young Families. Dean began his ministry at BCBC on August 16, 2008.

Pastoral Care Team. While the deacons participate in pastoral care, by virtue of their office, which includes support to the pastor, a specially trained pastoral care group was established in 1986 in the Orleans area. This was an inter-church initiative by Orleans United Church, St. David's Anglican Church, St. Joseph's Roman Catholic Church and BCBC.[68] Pastoral care workers were given 10 weeks of training.[69] Half of the weekly sessions were devoted to "listening skills" in different situations.[70] The Pastoral Care team reported as their mission "to keep in touch with the church family through the good times and those tough hurtful times and to be a comfort to them in prayer and assistance during difficult times." The church list is divided up between the team members so that each family will be prayed for individually and in group meetings. If the team members become aware of special needs they inform the pastor and the deacons.[71] Jean Norman led the *Pastoral Care Team* and Carmen Paul the *Prayer Ministry*.

Administrative and Pastoral Support. In the beginning, BCBC had no paid administrative staff whatsoever. Apart from the Pastor, all were volunteers. However, as the volume of necessary administrative work grew, a number of part-time appointments became necessary. Thus Jen Messer was appointed as Administrative Officer and Kim Barriault as Assistant Administrative Officer with additional responsibility for music ministry support. While Jen Messer was on leave of absence, Kim acted in her position, with the assistance of Gail Lyons. At one point, Donna Zelmer provided support for the music ministry.

Summer Students. Up to two summer students were hired per year, over several years, with partial financial support from *Human Resources and Social Development Canada*, who performed administrative functions, as well as unique roles, such as participating in the operation of Daily Vacation Bible Schools. These summer students included some members of our own congregation, such as Kim Jen and Heather O'Brien. In 2003, Stephanie Richardson, a blind student from Ottawa University, worked as administrative assistant with special responsibility for developing a database for cataloguing BCBC library holdings. Virtually all other functions in the church are being performed by a large number of dedicated volunteers.

Chapter 6: Worship

The word "worship" means ascribing "worth" to God. The Bible describes worship in many ways. In the Old Testament, it included priestly service at the altar as well as prayer and praise as expressed in many psalms. In John 4: 23-24 and in Philippians 3:3, among many other New Testament passages, worship is described as a spiritual relationship with God. Other passages describe worship in terms of praise and glorification of God. In early church history, formal worship became known as *leiturgía*, which passed into the English language as *liturgy*. Christians worship in private, within the family, in small groups or publicly in formal services.

Among BCBC's original five ministry-oriented Commissions, the Worship Commission was placed first. This supremacy of worship among the other four ministry areas (preaching/mission/evangelism, teaching, fellowship and service) is also reflected in BCBC's mission statement: *To glorify God and to make and nurture disciples.*

While several years passed before the Worship Commission became operational, worship was already an important part of BCBC's first public service on September 23, 1984[72], which included prayer, hymns, a solo, other music and an announcement that a choir[73] would be formed shortly and that interested persons should contact Austin Moss.

BCBC's Constitution, which became effective at the time of the church's formal founding on September 20, 1987, contained, in Byelaw 8, the terms of reference of the Commission on Worship. In particular, in accordance with Article 4, the Commission was charged to *examine the following areas and make recommendations to Council:*

a) *the needs of the congregation with respect to worship, taking account of the needs of the children, youth and adults as well as shut-ins, formal and informal, and corporate and private worship, in the light of our Christian heritage;*
b) *the place of prayer in worship;*
c) *the role of music in worship;*
d) *meaningful new worship experiences; [and]*
e) *means of educating the Congregation in worship. "*

Article 5 instructed the Commission to support the Pastor for planning the following functions: Covenant Sunday (Anniversary); Advent; Christmas; Lenten period; Easter; Pentecost; Thanksgiving; Communion services; baptismal services; and services of dedication and presentation.

In the first Commission Report[74] to the Annual Program Meeting on May 29, 1988, Gunter Rochow, its chairman, indicated that the Commission had held five meetings between December 9, 1987 and April 21, 1988. His report indicated that *"The Commission concentrated its initial activities on studying the nature of worship and its application at BCBC. "* The Commission's initial general conclusions were that:

- Worship is the ascription of worth to God;

- it is a response stemming from the worshipper's personal experience of God as loving Father and ultimate authority;

- in practice, worship is dialogue between the worshipper and his God in which God speaks through the Scriptures and his chosen ministers, and the worshipper responds to God's love, addresses himself to God in praise, confesses his sin, receives God's forgiveness, interceded for his fellowmen and commits himself to God's service;

- worship can be formal and corporate as in a church service, or informal and private as in personal devotions and, generally, in the life that is focused on God;

- the types of worship can vary in accordance with many factors, such as the ecclesiastical tradition of the majority of worshippers, the age range and age distribution of the congregation, and the resources at the disposal of the worshippers, such as the general facilities (buildings), musical skills and instruments, books, and leadership of the congregation;

- worship is viewed as the supreme activity of the Church from which all other activities stem and into which they flow.

The initial Commission report also drew some specific conclusions about the preferred structure of the worship service, suggesting that it be:

- a unified service in which all parts hang together around a central theme,
- a service where the parts focus on God, and
- an experience that is, to the extent possible, uninterrupted by extraneous activities, such as announcements (which should precede or follow the worship service).

Other recommendations of the first Commission report were:

- that the offering be a part of the worshipper's self-offering and commitment to God, not just a collection;
- that the external environment should be supportive of the worship experience, by assuring silence before the service begins, silence during the postlude to facilitate personal reflection, avoidance and screening out noises from adjoining facilities; and
- that members should be encouraged to participate actively in the worship experience through singing, responsive readings or by leading parts of the worship experience.

While the Worship Commission tried its best in the earlier years, it was handicapped as long as BCBC did not have its own accommodation. Consequently, the Commission became more consistently active after BCBC moved into its own Phase I building. Over the years, the Commission held team meetings to guide the worship team members, to set goals, discuss concerns, explore ideas,

study together, foster devotions and pray. By 2009 that led to the formulation of the elements for the following statement: *The purpose of the Bilberry Creek Baptist Church Worship Commission is to prepare to lead the congregation in worship and glorify God through music, prayer, reading of the Word, and various expressions of praise and adoration, in order to fulfill its mission of glorifying God, and making and nurturing disciples.*

Corporate Worship

At BCBC corporate worship is family worship, geared to adults, youth and children. As such it blends elements for all ages, using some traditional hymns as well as newer music that appeals especially to the younger generation. In 1996/1997 there was some discussion about offering two services, one for families and their children, and another for the older generation.[75] Wisely that concept was not pursued, since there are many experiences in other churches where the notion of two parallel services differentiated by age became divisive.

The church leadership also expressed the view that *our belief in the priesthood of all believers is evidenced in our corporate worship, where we try to involve many members to use their spiritual gifts.*[76] This thrust is reflected in a highly participatory approach that brings together adults and youth, choir members, instrumental musicians as well as persons reading the Scriptures and offering prayer.

As for involving youth, during the winter of 1992-1993, the first Youth Service was held, with all youth participating and Tim Avery leading. [77] That experience has become an annual event. To help children in their worship experience, children stories often involved Joy Huettner with her puppet "Willie" and ventriloquism dialogue. Betty Stephens, assisted by her husband Campbell, had developed a unique style in telling her many children stories. Jonathan Rendall and others were also frequent participants.

Worship leaders had always planned worship as part of the Sunday service. Fred and Rene Weiss are referenced in an extant Church Bulletin as worship leaders on October 11, 1987. During the same time period, and even earlier,[78] Robyn and David Oickle also participated, often to Robyn's guitar accompaniment. The worship leader's role became more formalized when the Commission on Worship organized *Worship Teams.* That was done after the congregation had moved into its own sanctuary at the end of 1993, which offered vastly better facilities. Over the years, apart from Don Collar, Doug McLean,

Sharon O'Brien, Elizabeth Allsopp, Kim Jen, Bob Dickinson, Bonnie Maitland, Doug Rochow and Colin Dickinson served as worship leaders. For some time, more than ten years later, the Worship Team held monthly DEEPP meetings (devotional, enjoying, eating, praying, praise)[79], but this was ultimately discontinued when turn-out continued to decline, for the simple reason that most choir members had to choose between priorities on their time.

Music

Music was a part of the worship experience of all ages. The Psalms refer to musical accompaniment on harps, flutes, lyres and other instruments. When BCBC began its public services, Bonnie Maitland provided piano accompaniment[80] for congregational singing. Extant early church bulletins indicate that Pam McPhail was the pianist on January 27, 1985, Mr. Desmond Hassell (the organist from First Baptist Church) on March 24, Betty Stevens on March 31 (and on unknown earlier occasions, usually when Austin Moss or a quartet

Box 6. He Is My Rock
Words and Music by Doug Rochow, ©1996

He is my rock, a firm foundation
He is my rock, and cannot be removed
He is my Lord, and I know
No storm can ever shake
A peaceful home to make
He is my Lord
Chorus:
He is my rock, He is. He is my strength
He is my shield. On Him I depend.
In Him I place my hope. He is my Lord.

He is my strength, when crushed beneath my pain
He is my strength, to carry on today.
He is my Lord, and I know
His arms are large enough
For Him nothing's too rough
He is my Lord (chorus)

He is my shield, when danger's at my door
He is my shield, He guides me through the storm
He is my Lord, and I know
The power of His hand
My foes He will disband
He is my Lord (chorus)

He is my hope, for life that never ends
He is my hope, He is my constant joy
He is my Lord, and I know
Jesus may come today
To take us all away.
He is our Lord.

sang) and Rosanne DeVries (from Eastview Baptist Church) on Easter Sunday, April 7, 1985, as well as on several other occasions. Heather Vos is first mentioned in the bulletins as pianist on May 19, 1985 and then again on June 30, 1985, as well as on subsequent Sundays. Early in the Collars' ministry, Cathy Collar organized a roster of about six pianists and participated herself frequently in providing musical accompaniment during worship services.

Vocal music also existed from the beginning, with Austin Moss offering a solo during the first service on September 23, 1984 and a Ladies Trio,[81] consisting of Miriam Sears, Pam McPhail and Corinne Potvin, singing during the second service. Many others followed, as for example, duets by Bonnie Maitland and Lisee Kiar,[82] Lisee Kiar and Cathy Collar,[83] as well as solos by Françoise de St-Jean.[84] A feast of music occurred on the first Anniversary Sunday[85] on September 22, 1985 when *Children of Bilberry* had a "Butterfly Song", *Puppeteers* (Kristen Newsham, Ruth and Karen Turle) sang "Amen, Praise the Lord", a *Carpenters' Quartet* followed, and Françoise de St-Jean sang a solo.

Members of the congregation not only participated in vocal music, but also composed Christian music. Douglas Rochow wrote several pieces that are still used in BCBC worship. One of these, *He is My Rock*, arose out of the depth of a family crisis. He wrote:

> "I waited patiently for the LORD; he turned to me and heard my cry. He lifted me out of the slimy pit, out of the mud and mire; he set my feet on a rock and gave me a firm place to stand. He put a new song in my mouth, a hymn of praise to our God. Many will see and fear and put their trust in the LORD." Psalm 40:1-3

I had been married for five years when, in November 1990, my comfortable family life came to a crashing halt. All it took was one phone call, one two minute call, to transform my wife from someone I knew to a stranger who would have to be hospitalized on and off for years to come. I would like to say I waited patiently for the Lord, but I can't. I was angry and confused. This was not the life I envisioned for my family. I was angry at God. I knew Him but it seemed He let me down. I stopped going to church thinking "why bother?"

People from church started to bring dinners for my family. I said to myself "Hmm … that was nice of them." One Friday evening when my wife was in hospital, I worried all night about how I was going to clear the foot [of] snow that was expected to fall from our long driveway. I could not leave three small children by themselves in the house nor leave them in the snow while I cleared the driveway. I did not know what to do. I just fretted. Yes, it had snowed during the night but, in the morning, my driveway was cleared. I could not believe it. I said to myself "Hmm … maybe God does care for me after all." I found out several months later that a neighbour, four or five houses down, had a heart attack just before Christmas and his son gave him a snowblower for Christmas. He decided to clear my driveway. Why? Why did he come to me? How could he have known my need that day? Did God plant a seed in his heart? Hmm. I started developing a peace within my soul. God had moved me. He had lifted me up out of the mud and mire. I started to feel secure in spite of the turmoil I found myself in. I know now that people wore out their knees praying for my family and me ... and for that, I am forever grateful.

I know now that: "In the same way, the Spirit helps us in our weakness. We do not know what we ought to pray for, but the Spirit himself intercedes for us with groans that words cannot express." Romans 8:26. God did restore my family, albeit not as I had envisioned it. He renewed my strength as I began to lean more and more on Him. He kept our family safe from many flaming arrows of the evil one with His shield constantly on guard. Most of all He renewed my faith and hope for an eternal life with Him. Several years later I came across Psalm 56 that says: "When I am afraid, I will trust in you. In God, whose word I praise, in God I trust; I will not be afraid. What can mortal man do to me?" Psalm 56:3-4. "What can mortal man do to me?" Nothing. Live or die, I will be with the Lord. Thank you, Jesus, for your mercies are new every morning.

The musical resources for worship developed over time. While the congregation worshipped in the schools, a piano was readily available. That changed when the Phase I building became available. To meet the initial need, Mr. Karl and Mrs. Annie Rochow, Gunter Rochow's parents, donated their Baldwin home organ. BCBC also benefitted from the presence on the same premises of *Music Alive*, Bonnie Maitland's music school, which permitted the congregation to use her electronic and acoustic pianos. Later, Elaine and Arthur Eckert became aware of the availability of a grand piano. To acquire it, both they and Olivet Baptist Church in Sarnia provided the necessary funds. Betty and Brian Richardson (Bonnie Maitland's twin sister and brother-in-law) played a major role in that they suggested to Olivet that some of that Church's remaining funds, after it closed, be donated as a contribution towards the purchase of the grand piano. Apart from piano accompaniment, many other instruments were used in worship. Jack Shearer was the first flute player, followed later by Crystal Thieringer. Suzanne Martin and Claire Rendall also played the flute. Guitar players included Don Collar in the early years, and later Brad Collar and Donald Vinette. New music is introduced either through instrumental music or through special music led by the Worship team.

The Phase I accommodation also led to other enhancements of the worship experience, such as the installation of overhead projection facilities and the purchase of a CCLI licence to be able to use a wide range of Christian music and words. When the church purchased drums in 2000, it shared the cost with the French congregation. Similarly, the French congregation contributed to the construction of the sound booth. Robert Allsop, Bing Hum, and later Barry Francis and Don Vinette undertook the necessary wiring for music delivery. The new technology required a great deal of learning and fine-tuning.

Brian Martin was the first media person, followed by Nicola Martin, who fulfilled this role faithfully over several years – for every practice and every Sunday! Nevertheless, some problems with sound remained, were frustrating and not easy to fix, partially due to older equipment. How the team led worship changed to some extent over time, as instruments were added and microphones, sound boards and monitors were used. The function of monitors is important, since it allows the singers and musicians to hear themselves, since the sound comes back to them.

Under the leadership of Janice Rochow, and Pam McPhail before her, the choir participated in worship on about a monthly basis and on special occasions, such as Easter, Covenant Sunday (Anniversary), Thanksgiving, Advent and Christmas). Early choir members included Marguerite Hum, Cheryl Jones, Janice Rochow, Elizabeth Allsopp, Donna Zelmer, Bonnie Maitland, Donna Beaulieu and Doug Rochow and later Joanne Rochow. A children's choir was started in the late 1990s, and on several occasions the BCBC choir and the choir of the French congregation join their efforts in a bilingual ministry. On occasion, sacred dance was used in worship. Some of the participants were Joanna Demers, Emilie Plows, and Natalie Beaubien from the French congregation. Hymn sing evenings typically occur in the fall. JoAnn Guitard contributed to the décor of the sanctuary by making the Banner King of Kings".

Since about 2007, the Worship Commission encouraged prayer before the worship service to ask for God's blessing and strength for the Worship Team and for individual members of the Team.

Chapter 7: Preaching, Mission and Evangelism

Originally, Preaching, Evangelism and Mission were addressed in one Commission, because these three functions shared the Greek New Testament concept of *kerygma*, i.e. the announcing of the *Good News* of salvation, as referenced, among other passages, in Matthew 12:41, Luke 11:32, Romans 16:25 and 1. Corinthians 1:21.

Early in 2002, the Pastor "met with the Commission and discussed his concern that our church does not have enough outreach into the community, such as seminars [or a] fall fair". "The Commission members were overwhelmed with the idea of being responsible for planning large-scale events."[86] The Commission and the Pastor agreed that more thought was needed. As a result, the Commission undertook a planning session during the summer months and made other attempts to address the Pastor's concerns. Nevertheless, ultimately the result was that local evangelism was dropped from the Commission's responsibility, focusing primarily on "mission" [overseas], as had been its practice all along. To fill the local void, beginning in 2006, a separate *Evangelism Commission* was established, which was formally recognized in 2008[87]. Douglas Rochow, then its chairman, participated in October 2007 in the Billy Graham School of Evangelism, St. Andrews, NB[88].

The *Mission Commission* acted as a link between the congregation and overseas missionaries, including, but not limited to missionaries sent out by *Canadian Baptist Ministries*, and focusing mainly on those with whom BCBC maintained a special partner relationship. These missionaries included the Faddegon's, for whom the congregation maintained repeated prayer support while their daughter Jessica underwent cancer treatment in Canada. The missionary partners also included Carl and Cathy Janzen and Laurence and Kathy Cheveldayoff in Brazil, the Ho family in China, and the Deneut and Godwin families in Belgium. The Mission Commission not only reported at BCBC about overseas missionaries, but in 1997-1998, Helen Meubus, a member of the Mission Commission, and her husband Yves visited the

Deneut's in Belgium. Some other BCBC members did likewise. Thus, in 2003 Jun Zhang, Frank Liu, and their sons went to Chengdu, China, for Christmas to visit with the Ho family.

Brief presentations known as "Mission Spots" were frequent aspects of Sunday services, in which a Commission member shared news from the field and encouraged prayer for particular aspects of ministry.

The *Mission Commission* was also involved with short-term missionaries[89], among them several BCBC members. These included Kim Jen[90] who participated in Medical Mission to Haiti in March 2000, Emily Camire [91] in Leeds, England, in 2002, Heather Bunning, working with the *Campus Crusade for Christ* in Tanzania in 2003[92] and in China[93] in 2005, Andrea Rochow with Baptist youth in the Dominican Republic in March 2005, as well as with street people in Montreal and Toronto, Joanna Demers[94], who went to Africa, Elie Atallah[95] serving in the Czech Republic in 2006, Alison Hunting (Allsopp) and her husband Alastair, in Japan,[96] and in Canada, Jillian Zelmer who was involved with *Intervarsity Christian Fellowship*, including a mission assignment in Ecuador[97], and Bethanna Cavey who worked with *Urban Promise* in Toronto, a non profit charitable organization that is dedicated to meeting the needs of children, youth and their families in risk communities.[98]

The *Mission Commission* also recognized BCBC members who worked abroad in secular functions, where they also engaged in "mission" activities. In 1991, Waldo Rochow was asked to comment publicly about the work of his parents in Venezuela. Similarly, when Jacques Marcheterre served on two occasions with the RCMP in Haiti, and on one occasion in Guinea, West Africa, he was a "missionary" apart from his police duties, working with local churches (see Box 7). In 1998 both Jacques Marcheterre and Gunter and Reinhilde Rochow were recognized in the Mission Spot[99] regarding their work in Haiti and Indonesia, respectively. Apart from Gunter Rochow's development work under a CIDA subcontract in Indonesia, both Reinhilde Rochow and he were active as co-chairs in providing leadership to the Outreach Committee of *All Saints Anglican Church* in Jakarta. That role involved about thirty projects including orphanages, Bible translation, radio ministry, and other types of service. BCBC as a whole recognized this role of its members by offering commissioning prayers during the Sunday service before their departure.

Box 7. Jacques Marcheterre in Haiti
In 1995, while in active service with the RCMP, I volunteered for my first United Nations Mission to Haiti. I did not know it at the time, but this was going to be the first of eventually four such UN missions in that country. This first mission was for a duration of six months. I left Canada on July 3rd with seven RCMP colleagues, full of excitement as we embarked on this adventure together. Only one among us had previous UN mission experience, having served in Namibia in 1989. For some reason, that did not seem to have prepared him much for

---

what we would experience in Haiti. Our tons of kit and equipment would not compensate for our little knowledge of the country, its people, its history, its culture, its climate. After another week of training and orientation by the UN in Haiti, we were posted to various communities throughout the country. Three of us were sent to Mirebalais located 50 km north of Port-au-Prince, just a short 3 ½ hour drive. I was to take the command of that post and open its first detachment.

Soon after my arrival in Mirebalais, I met Pastor Yves Valmy, who was pastoring l'Eglise Baptiste des Rachetés (Baptist Church of the Redeemed), a congregation of about 25 or 30 people. They did not have a dedicated hall or place of worship other than the yard behind the pastor's very modest two room rented house. I began to attend the Sunday morning services, outside under the shade of huge trees, sitting on long wooden benches. Everything was different and unfamiliar. Of course, I was the only one looking so different. It must have been the uniform. I was often an attraction for the children specially when they warmed up and got close enough to touch a "blanc" (literally; white, creole for stranger). The brave ones would rub the hair on my arms and smile. Some were happy to spend the whole service right next to their new friend, Blanc. What was not so different were the songs they sang, in Creole of course and some in French, but the same tunes I knew. The folks were surprised I could sing along. I remember the blessing of knowing I could worship God so far away from home, in such a different land, with some of His people. I suppose I had always known intellectually that God had saints throughout His creation, but it became more real to me. So, for as many Sunday mornings as I could take the time (working seven day a week with no days off) I attended the Sunday School and the worship services at l'Eglise Baptiste des Rachetés. I became friends with Pastor Yves and his family and on occasion, during the week, I stopped by for a visit. Pastor Yves also returned the visits once or twice a week at my house in the evenings. I so welcomed the mutual encouragement and the Christian fellowship.

Out of my comparative wealth, I was able to help Pastor Yves and his family financially. By local standards, they were living like most others, in poverty. His only source of income was what the other poor of the congregation could afford to spare. By material standards, it was not much. After a short while, pastor Yves was able to move his family into a newer, somewhat larger house a short distance away. This little house had more living space for the family and even had a room at the front where the church was crammed on Sunday mornings. It was terribly hot and had poor ventilation. I much preferred meeting outside in the shade and hot breeze. Pastor Yves was convinced the new arrangement was better as he could now house the congregation. He was certainly right when it poured.

On one occasion, I asked Pastor Yves what the most practical help he and his congregation could receive. I knew it was a loaded question and it could have gone anywhere. It could have ended up in disappointment to both of us by raising his expectations and by my not being able to meet them. I was surprised when he answered that the people needed shoes. Some walked great distances and did not have adequate footwear, children and adults alike. Shoes, even used shoes, were not readily available in that village and it was not practical to take everyone to Port-au- Prince. Knowing that we all had a surplus of shoes in our closets, it was just a matter of collecting them and transporting them to Mirebalais. In addition to the request for shoes, over time, I had had a conversation with Pastor Yves regarding his desire and ability to garden, raising some vegetables and some animals to provide for his family. He simply did not have the means to get started. He could not afford to rent the land and had no tools.

Consequently, during my subsequent trip home on leave, I informed the BCBC congregation of the need and asked for donations of used shoes; ladies, men's and children shoes. The donations of shoes poured in filling over four 4 cubic feet packing boxes. In addition to the shoes, many made cash donations to help Pastor Yves and his family. The number of shoes far exceeded the immediate need of the small congregation. Pastor Yves knew the people well and distributed the excess of shoes among them. They could sell the extra pairs and generate some extra cash. The cash donations were used to rent a plot of land, purchase necessary gardening tools as well as some goats and chicken providing a meaningful start toward providing for the needs of his family. The garden plot was of quite significant size. I remember thinking I would have wanted a tractor to work it if it had been mine, but Pastor Yves had managed to share the use of the plot with some other folks from the congregation. It was well used and the blessing had already multiplied. Returning home in December 1993 after six months of UN service, I remember the same thought I had had on my way there. In our week of pre-deployment orientation and training, the Haiti Ambassador to Canada came to address our group prior to departure. He thanked us for volunteering and asked us, not so much to bring his people out of poverty, but to help his people get out of misery. I remain thankful to this day for the opportunity I have had to travel to Haiti and meet brothers and sisters in Christ and, with the contribution of my church at BCBC, assist in a very practical way a part of the Body that was in need. In the Name of Jesus, thank you again. Jacques

At home, the *Mission Commission* supported the *Miriam Centre*[100], a place where women of all ages can receive whatever help they need during a pregnancy. The Commission also looked at *World Vision's* "Women at Risk"[101] program, which addresses the needs of women around the world who have been widowed or separated from their husbands and who are at great risk of spending the rest of their lives in refugee camps, where they must sleep, cook and raise their children.

The *Evangelism Commission* focused on outreach in the Orleans area, among other activities, through the prison ministry[102] at the *Ottawa-Carleton Regional Detention Centre,* in which Douglas Rochow, along with Jenelyn Umapas and Cherrie Bulahan from BCBC and Louis Nguyen from *Église Évangélique Baptiste d'Orléans* , participated regularly with representatives from other churches (See Boxes 8A and 8B). This outreach is based on the Alpha program.[103] One of the outcomes of this ministry was the *Ex-Offenders Friendly Church Project*, which aimed at supporting ex-offenders within a church after their release.

Box 8A. Prison Ministry. Its Background and Context

Bilberry's involvement in prison ministry at the Ottawa Carleton Regional Detention Centre began in 2006 following the creation of the Evangelism Commission. Doug Rochow, as chair of the Commission, suggested that Bilberry consider a prison ministry given the fact that the detention centre is not too far from the church. In a meeting with the prison chaplain, Carl Wake, it was suggested that we could tap into the Alpha Canada program already in existence at the detention centre. That program had been running for approximately five years at that time. Cherrie Bulahan, Jenelyn Umapas, Dan Dupuis and Louis Nguyen had been part of the prison alpha team at various times. The program is essentially the same as is offered outside of prison with some special adaptations due to the transient nature of our guests (inmates). Guests are free to discuss questions of Christian faith and explore answers in a group setting. Many guests have given their hearts to Christ through the exposure they received in this programme. In June 2007, we were allowed to offer baptism by immersion to twelve inmates who requested to be baptized. By the end of 2009, more than ninety men and women had followed Christ in baptism. Baptisms in Prison are offered twice per year to guests who have decided to follow Jesus and wish to take this step of obedience to Him.

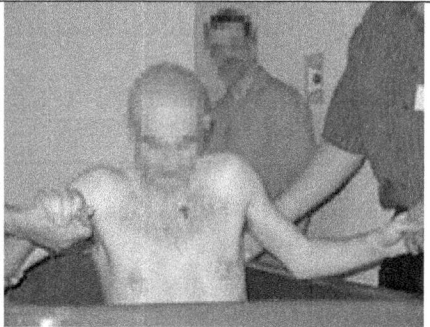

Chaplain Carl Wake (left) with nine baptismal candidates, and volunteers Doug Rochow and Max B. (right)

The strength of this ministry lies in the genuine love and concern (something that has often been lacking since early childhood) that is offered to our guests by volunteers from a variety of Christian traditions; The focus is on Christ and His mission to seek and save the lost and His plan for salvation and everlasting life for those who believe in Him. Emphasis is also placed on the need for aftercare. Attendance is voluntary and guests choose to give up "yard time" in order to take part in the programming.

In addition to teaching about the all-important relationship with Jesus Christ, the program promotes local services such as MAP Reintegration, a community chaplaincy (which stands for Mentorship, Aftercare, Presence), which assists our guests with basic needs for shelter, work, etc. while providing mentorship during their reintegration into society. This mentorship role is a major player in reversing recidivism rates. Furthermore, those guests who are determined to make amends are encouraged to participate in the Collaborative Justice Program at the Ottawa Court House.

Box 8B. Prison Ministry. The Testimony of an Inmate (2009)

I felt unloved, unwanted and so empty my whole life. I felt I never had a purpose, meaning or any faith. As far as I can remember, I was always in trouble. I lied, cheated and was so full of denial. I was given many chances and blew them all. I couldn't tell a lie from the truth.

I was thrown out of the house at 13 and got into so much trouble. I felt and believed the world owed me a living. Reform school, psychiatric wards and incarceration were quite common for me. No one knew what to do with me, although they tried. I was so self-centered, selfish, stubborn and full of self pity. I firmly believed God was out to punish me. I was physically, sexually and mentally abused. Many times I just wanted to die. Happiness was for others … not me.

An amazing thought came to mind: Why not sincerely ask God for help? I didn't know how to lift myself up and didn't have the courage to end it. What did I have to lose by asking God for help? Absolutely nothing. I started with prayer and daily devotional readings. I realized I failed … Not God. He was carrying me through every trial and tribulation waiting for me to simply surrender.

I now pray for more faith. I feel so free and content like never before. Today I am eager to learn more about God the Father, His son Jesus and the Holy Spirit. I realize I need much work as God continues to change me but, as long as I look to His light, I will get there. Currently, I know God's Holy Spirit is within me because, for the very first time, I have sincere compassion, love and hope for my fellow human beings and my journey is no longer without purpose. I owe God everything.

My new life is about knowing more about God's Word and what can I do to for others to make a difference. I know that I may fall short but I have a sincere eagerness to be humble, teachable and loving. For the very first time it is not all about me. Where I have been is no longer as important as where I am going.

So for those who may feel lost, open your heart and let God in. You may be surprised but not sorry. The Bible says, all who call on the name of the Lord will be saved.

I had to finally surrender to God and be honest with myself. Give God a chance.

Comment from a Prison Ministry member: These words ring true and AJ's demeanor rings true as well. A few weeks ago, a guard mentioned that there has traditionally been one riot every four years at OCDC, but that there has not been a riot for over eight years. The Alpha program has been operating at OCDC for about nine years. Could this be due to the Holy Spirit's presence at OCDC? Hmm...

There were also other occasional events such as community visitation and the annual "Santa's Parade of Lights"[104] for which BCBC, in collaboration with *Église Évangélique Baptiste d'Orléans,* repeatedly entered a spectacular float that focused on the meaning of Christmas. The 2006 parade had an impact that lasted for several months. The float's message was "Come to Jesus to Live". The Holy Spirit was definitely felt at the parade, as the crowd was hushed while the float went by. Many letters to the editor of *The Star*[105], discussed, between November and March, the controversial issue of public expression of faith.

Box 9. The Parade of Lights

I Love to Tell the Story of Jesus and His Love

The 2000-Year-Old Stories of Jesus Retold in Light and Sound at the "Santa's Parade of Lights" in Orleans, Ontario

By Doug Rochow

Twenty-three people from Bilberry Creek Baptist Church and its sister French congregation, Eglise Evangelique Baptiste D'Orleans, worked day and night for almost three weeks to prepare its first entry in the "Santa's Parade of Lights" held on November 25, 2006. This float was one of seven floats with Christian themes. There were 43 floats in total. Pictures along side of the float told the story of Jesus from His birth to ascension while people on the float sang "What's Most Important at Christmas?," a song I wrote with Kelly Wiseman, from our church, several years ago. The music was amplified through speakers and was complemented with verbal confirmation that "Jesus loves you and wants you and your family to have a blessed Christmas." We knew our entry had the potential to be controversial as it was likely the most evangelical one. It was a phenomenal success! The local community newspaper has been buzzing for more than three months now, with articles about whether or not people should keep their religion to themselves, the majority supporting religious expression. I purposefully did not write until recently, as I wanted to hear other opinions first (see my letter on the next page).

I have had such a strong feeling that God is going to do something incredibly great and wonderful this year, not just in our community but in our country, and world. I encourage everyone to share the Gospel of Jesus Christ. Put on your creative thinking caps and purposefully make opportunities to meet your neighbours, colleagues and friends. Find ways to purposefully share God's love with others through simple and repetitive acts of kindness: holding a community barbeque early this summer, shovelling the neighbour's driveway or cutting their lawn, helping them plant a garden, babysitting their children, bringing them a plate of cookies or whatever … the sky's the limit!

Be Bold. Be Strong …for the Lord Your God is With You!

But, do so with gentleness wrapped in God's love.
He will bless these little things in ways we cannot fathom.

It was comforting to see that many of the commentators still recognized the freedom of religious expression. Only God knows how many people may have been moved to enter into a relationship with Him, but it is certain that the seed was planted.

The visit of the *Cambridge Kiwanis Boys' Choir* and *Young Men's Chorus*, on May 12, 2007[106], unexpectedly became an evangelistic event. The concert attracted many people from the community. The fact that the *Henry Larsen Elementary School Choir* joined the boys on one number, meant that many parents, who may or may not attend church, had an opportunity to hear the gospel message in song. Another such event occurred in August 2009, when the *Jeonju Ambassador Singers* from South Korea presented a concert at BCBC as part of their Canadian Tour.[107]

Before the formal establishment of the current *Evangelism Commission* in 2008, there is already evidence of extensive evangelistic activity. Nevertheless, it is clear that BCBC largely participated in the planning that was undertaken by other organizations rather than develop its own church-specific outreach plan. Examples of that activity include the following. In 1988, 3,000 flyers were distributed in the community, and over 1,500 in new communities east of Tenth Line. In 1992-1993, "Focus on Jesus" flyers were distributed. [108] In 1993, BCBC participated in the Jesus Video Campaign[109], involving for BCBC the allotment of a block of 500 homes. BCBC began to use the Alpha program in 1997, after Pastor Don and some deacons participated in an Alpha supper at St. Helen's Anglican Church. [110] BCBC also participated in the Billy Graham Crusade and Operation Andrew in June 1998[111]. The *Hope 2000 Evangelistic Campaign,*[112] consisting of English and French door-to-

door community visitation, was undertaken with the participation of the Young People and the Youth Pastor of Forward Baptist Church of Cambridge, Ontario; about 150 people took part.

Box 10. Report to Team on Canada Day Witness on Petrie Island in 2009[113]

In 2007, God gave us favor before the officials of Orleans. This was an opportunity to serve the community on Canada Day at Petrie Island. The community has a tradition of celebrating Canada Day on the beach. 12,000 - 18,000 people usually attend. We did face painting, church VBS advertisement, cleanup volunteering and even some open air preaching. Since that time, the organizers continued to invite us every year.

This year, two days before Canada Day, I was ready to give up. All our face painting materials were nowhere to be found. Our churches' banners were missing. The number of volunteers could be counted on one hand. Cancelling our participation [might be] our last chance to save face. But, read: Is. 41:10; Phil 4:13; 1. Cor. 15:58; Heb. 12:3; Num 23:19; ...2. Cor. 4:5. We don't go around preaching ourselves; we preach Christ Jesus, the Lord.... God reminded me of the necessity of obedience and of trusting Him with everything. Rom 8:32, since God did not spare even his own Son, but gave him up for us all, won't God, who gave us Christ, also give us everything else? With this refocus on Christ, we continued working preparing for Canada Day. God surprised us with so many awesome things on July 1st:

01h30 - Finished new banners. Interesting fact: Instead of putting our churches' names and addresses, the main, the poster simply said: "Free Face Painting courtesy of Jesus".
02h30 - Found red and white paint supply. Praise God!
09h30 - Found paint brushes. Praise Him again!
10h00 - Prayer
10h50 - Ready and heading out for Petrie Island
17h30 - Closing for the day

On July 1st, we were blessed to see God provide more volunteers than expected. They came from SKETCH, a start-up company working with children and teenagers of Orleans and from the Muslim community. It was our first time working together with them. I am sure God has more plans for us to meet them again. We were not prepared for open air preaching, but we had many encounters with parents and obviously painted children. You should see the smile from children's faces…. Now thinking back about this event, I am sad that I will probably never see these people at a Sunday church service. But, at the same time, I thank God for this opportunity to serve them. For one day, we were Jesus' hands and feet amongst people. It was truly God's miracles during this event. Even the rain at the right time helped us to bind with the community (our face painting tent was the largest shelter on site) and to clean the next day (the rain washed away most of the dirt). Praise to God for His many promises from His Word, for His provision for everything from material to last minute volunteers; for 458 faces painted; for 20 new registrations for our church VBS; for a continued relationship with organizers from city of Orleans; for a new relationship with SKETCH; and for new relationship with Muslim community.

Thank you for your support prayers.
Your servants in Christ,
Louis Nguyen
Église Évangélique Baptiste d'Orléans, Leader for joint EEBdO and BCBC Team

The "Let's Go to Church" month for January 2000[114], was organized by the *Greater Orleans Ministerial Association* (GOMA). In 2002, the churches in the community connected with those who attended the *International Plowing Match*[115] in Navan, which included the use of a Christian Farmers' Outreach Tent, at which walking sticks were presented to several hundred men, women and children who listened to a brief two minute presentation of the Gospel. 6,000 presentations were made, as a result of which 600 requested follow-up, and 14 of these were assigned to BCBC. In 2002, under Barry Pugh's leadership, BCBC, along with other sponsors, participated in setting up large uniform tulip sculptures[116] in downtown Ottawa in front of City Hall, as part of the annul Tulip Festival in May. BCBC's tulip represented "Christian Life in the Community" and referenced Psalm 133:1. On Canada Day 2002, *Église Évangélique Baptiste d'Orléans* (EEBdO) and BCBC set up a Christian Tent[117] in Fallingbrook. This led to annual events at Canada Day celebrations when Louis Nguyen of EEBdO approached the organizers of the Canada Day celebrations at Petrie Island. Douglas Rochow reported that "typically, we have painted over 300 faces each year… [and] we offered a prayer booth in case any people would like to have a time of prayer."[118]

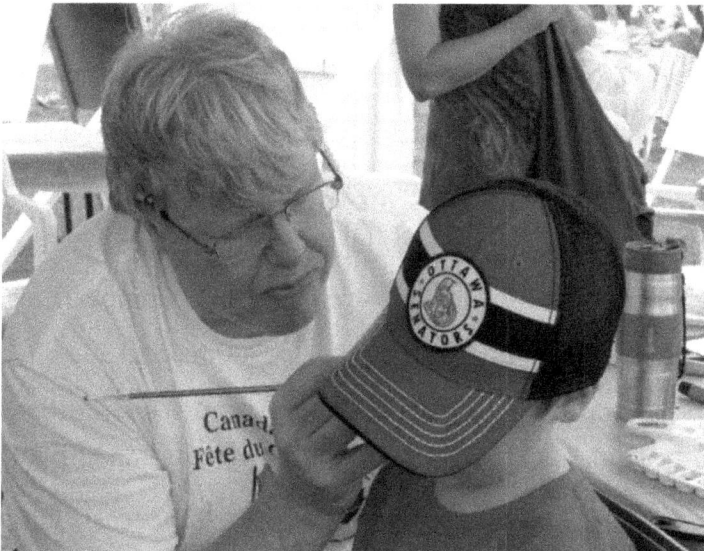

In practice, the *preaching* aspect of *kerygma* had never been addressed by the Commission on *Preaching, Mission and Evangelism*, as it had been intended originally. Instead, *preaching,* insofar as it relates to one of the roles of the Pastor, is a part of the general support to the pastoral ministry provided by the Board of Deacons. The Commission did not address, as had been hoped, planning for preaching functions by members of the congregation in outreach or other ministries, such as providing pulpit supply in churches without pastors, conducting worship services in seniors' residences and nursing homes, as well as pursuing other opportunities that might present themselves. In spite of the fact that the Commission did not take up this dimension of its mandate, this intended function was executed in an ad hoc fashion as several BCBC members rose to the different occasions as they emerged.

Several BCBC members provided supply preaching in other churches. As Lay-Preacher licensed by CBOQ and BCBC,[119] Campbell Stephens, together with his wife Betty, preached frequently in several churches in the Ottawa area, as well as in senior residences such as Glebe Centre, Laurier Manor and Rothwell Heights. Campbell and Betty Stephens and Austin Moss participated in a Pittston United Church[120] Anniversary Service in 1988. In 1989 Austin Moss participated in services at South Gower Baptist Church,[121] which Gunter Rochow led. Over several years, Gunter Rochow also led occasional summer services at a community church at Blue Sea Lake, Quebec, which was sponsored by the Anglican Church of Canada. Special preaching and teaching events, which involved Gunter Rochow in 2004-2005, were the 100th anniversaries of the Prado Baptist Church in La Paz and the Calama Baptist Church in Cochabamba, respectively, both in Bolivia, where Gunter and Reinhilde Rochow served as missionaries from 1966-1971. In 2006 Gunter Rochow preached at the 50th Anniversary of *Zion Community Baptist Church* in Edmonton, where he was the first Student Pastor before the new church could call a regular pastor.

BILBERRY – *A Seed in Good Soil*

Chapter 8: Teaching

Teaching was an important function in Jesus' ministry and in that of the early church, as described in John 7:16f, Acts 2:42, 1. Corinthians 14:6, and 2. Timothy 4:2. In the early Church the body of Christian Teaching was known as *didaché*. In its original conception, the *Teaching Commission* was responsible for overseeing the work of the Sunday School for children, youth and adults, Junior Worship, midweek Bible studies and other unique opportunities for teaching and learning.

Along with worship and preaching/mission/evangelism, teaching started at the very beginning of BCBC's ministry. Even the get-acquainted service of praise and prayer on September 16, 1984 (i.e. on the Sunday before the official opening of BCBC) contained a "Sunday School". Nevertheless, although it had been planned since the beginning, to establish a *Teaching Commission,* this only came about after several years of incremental operation of its parts. That is quite understandable, since there were very few people to attend to the many urgent practical needs, and of necessity the focus had to be on the Sunday School. Perhaps, because of this iterative approach, different people using their knowledge and skills introduced approaches some of which were forgotten after they left. Thus, there is evidence of some discontinuity in programming, methods and materials, followed by new starts, but overall many dedicated people delivered the teaching function as a vibrant ministry.

In that context, David Oickle reported in 1988 that "the Sunday School had 59 registrants up to age 18. In addition to the basic David C. Cook curriculum of the Sunday School, the Junior Church offered preparation classes for the *Religion in Life Badge* and the *Grade V Religion Progression Program*. The Church recognized the accomplishment of Grade V students in Bible study by presenting a Bible to each, which was done for the first time in June 1988." David Oickle also indicated that: "The Education [sic.] Commission has started to oversee the growth of instruction to our church as a whole", beginning with "a series of taped instruction based entirely on live recordings of our Pastor's sermons" … "which will be available to those who have missed the service". "The Sunday School teachers' meetings lasted for two hours, where the first hour was devoted to Sunday School business and the routine of running programs, while

the second hour offered seminars designed to provide encouragement and growth for our teachers. In addition, plans were laid for a church library."

The first formal meeting of the *Teaching Commission* was held on August 26, 1996, with Gunter Rochow as Chair and Mary Wehrle, Rob Campbell and Esther Knorr as members, i.e. almost thirteen years after BCBC began and when the overall structure of commissions had been defined! In 1997, the Teaching Commission undertook an analysis of the Commission's work in terms of the three components of the Church's mission (i.e. glorifying God, making disciples and nurturing disciples) and identifying how these components were being addressed in the Sunday School (children, youth and adults), Bible Study (corporate and personal), counselling, discipleship, training for ministry (youth and adults), the Alpha project, community and social awareness and other Christian study. In his introduction to the subject, Gunter Rochow explained, among other things, that: "(1) The purpose of teaching is to contribute, in a planned and structured environment, to the spiritual development of the church family, comprising children, youth and adults; (2) the discussion of teaching should also comprise the commitment to promoting a learning culture, not limited to the efforts of the Sunday School, but including other weekday and weekend functions, as well as self-study through reading, computer-assisted learning and other means that are at our disposal; and (3) whatever functions are undertaken, should be goal-oriented, with specific learning outcomes." In October 1997, Mary Wehrle became the Chair, with Rob Campbell and Gunter Rochow continuing as members. One of the first activities of the new session of the Commission was to finalize the comprehensive review of programming within the context of BCBC's mission statement, which addresses the main components of "glorifying God, making disciples and nurturing disciples",[122] as well as analysing of the congregation's learning needs and the Commission's functions that had been begun earlier in that year.

Beth Porter-Jefferies was the longest serving Chair of the Teaching Commission, beginning in the fall of 1999[123]. She continued in that function until the present time, with a short interruption in 2003-2004, when the Teaching Commission was inactive. During that inactive year Douglas Rochow coordinated the work of the Sunday School. For a number of years Beth Porter-Jefferies shared her function with Sharon O'Brien until Sharon withdrew for health reasons. At that time,

Sharon Cavey joined Beth on the Teaching Commission. In retrospect, Beth wrote: "She [Sharon Cavey] brought a wealth of experience and energy to the ministry at a time when we were anticipating many changes."[124] During Beth's tenure, plans were laid for the development of a short course for newly-baptized members and other new members of the church along the lines of "Now What?" This was to be made available for the Pastor and Deacons for use in small group settings when appropriate. In the fall of 2009 this project was still on the Commission's "to do list".

The main functions of the *Teaching Commission* were to determine the needs of children, youth and adults for learning opportunities, administer the *Child Protection Policy*, staff the Sunday School, provide or identify training opportunities for teachers and officers, oversee the Church Library, procure teaching materials and to plan and support mission projects.

Over the years the curriculum changed. At one point the Sunday School used *David C. Cook* materials, except for the Adult class and one or two others, where the teachers liked to make their own. After a number of years the Teaching Commission changed the curriculum initially to Gospel Light and then to a BCBC in-house curriculum. Beth Porter-Jefferies explained the change as follows:

> I like the [David C.] Cook material, but after a few years, I began to wonder if we might look at some others for variety

and freshness. I also wanted to try to bring more consistency to our curriculum and get every teacher using material I could read in advance, and have available for a substitute when a teacher was sick. This proved a bit of a struggle for various reasons, but I did choose Gospel Light for the Elementary and Junior High grades as a well-designed program with fresh graphics and sound scope and sequence. After a few years, Sharon Cavey and I decided to try to plan to teach the younger grades the Old Testament narrative over a 3-4 year stretch, and she put together a curriculum herself because we could find no published one doing that in order. Also, because of the demographics of our Sunday School population and restrictions of space over the last few years, it made sense to combine the children from 6-11 years into one larger class, and that meant it wasn't possible to use the usual curricula from [David C.] Cook or Gospel Light with their breakdown into two-grade divisions. Older classes have continued to use different Bible or topical studies as we plan with their teachers.[125]

The choice of mission projects was in itself designed so as to help children understand that mission occurs both at home and abroad. Thus the mission offerings at Sunday School and in Junior Church were directed to projects within BCBC, the Ottawa area and elsewhere in Canada, as well as overseas. Projects within BCBC included: The Food Cupboard; money to purchase a banner to decorate our new church building; SumFun (Vacation Bible School); "Help Send a Kid to Camp" (a week at Camp Cherith for church family children); the Angel tree project at Christmas; and new Bibles for the church. Projects in Ottawa and elsewhere in Canada included: Help for Union Mission to rebuild after the fire; Capital City Mission; and "Help Turn on the Lights" in support of *Bethlehem Aboriginal Fellowship* (an inner-city clothing bank in Winnipeg). Projects abroad included: Sora India Chorus Books; Operation Eyesight; street children in Brazil; purchase of Sunday School materials for African Evangelical Churches; "Operation Christmas Child Shoe boxes"; Casa de la Amistad" (Bolivia), which is an outreach program for children who have to live in jail with an incarcerated parent; as well as a gift to the Sunday School of the Prado Baptist Church, La Paz, Bolivia, at the occasion of the Church's one hundredth anniversary.

Junior Church was delivered in many forms over the years. A very popular recent approach was "Adventure Bay". This is a program that teaches basic Christian values to children aged 4-10 using drama, games, songs, puppets, Bible stories and verses set aboard a ship sailing to various islands. It appeals to both churched and unchurched kids, and takes place at the same time as the worship service. It requires a stage and set, but also a regular cast and other rotating characters, costumes and props. It also requires a great deal of reworking over the year to tailor the lessons and logistics to suit the children's unique needs. To make Adventure Bay possible, Sharon and

Louis O'Brien had kindly donated a financial gift for refurbishing of the aging and dowdy module classrooms.[126] Some of BCBC's preteens and adults volunteered to help supervise the lively audience on a rotating basis. Several dedicated young adults and high school students developed the cast of characters week by week.

Some other Junior Church programs included a mission study about Bolivia and interesting things to see, led by Gunter Rochow, and monthly creative crafts were led by Miriam Sears.

During the summers, BCBC provided a Vacation Bible School or related program, at times as a church-specific program, or in collaboration with the *Ottawa Baptist Association* (OBA). In 1986 the program was delivered by BCBC youth assisted by a visiting *Youth Corp* team. In 1988, BCBC's program was delivered at the newly acquired *Bilberry Baptist Centre* on Innes Road. Subsequently, in collaboration with the *Ottawa Baptist Association*, a SumFun program was offered at Tucker House to which children were bused from all over the city, which proved to be a very costly undertaking. BCBC volunteers had participated in cleaning and painting Tucker House, to get it ready for the program. Kristen Newsham, John Wehrle, Beth and Tim Avery, as well as Karen Turle were involved as counselors. Four young people from *Bromley Road Baptist Church* and Jim Miller of *Open Air Campaigners*, helped the youth with SumFun. From a financial perspective, SumFun was not successful, and it was suspended when its board resigned. In 1991 the summer program was delivered in collaboration with *Child Evangelism Fellowship* and in August 1992 *Summer Jamboree* was offered. In preparation for the new program, a group of seven young people committed themselves to a seven-week training course for ministry to children that summer, led by Brian Jones, Bonnie Maitland and the Pastor. They were trained in storytelling, Scripture memorization, puppet ministry, and telling the Gospel through the "Wordless Book", i.e. a short story of God's salvation plan. The book was made up of different coloured pages, where green stands for God's earth, red stands for Christ shedding his blood, white stands for sins forgiven once we have accepted Christ as Saviour, and gold stands for streets in heaven. In 1994-1995 the OBA reintroduced SumFun with the expectation that the OBA churches would contribute voluntarily to its high cost. When that did not happen to a sufficient extent, the SumFun Board suggested a fee of $5.00 per child or $10.00 per family to help cover Bible materials and crafts. A highly imaginative summer program was offered in 1997, called "Sum Fun Safari Expeditions" with a new expedition every day for which the participants dressed up: South Pole, a desert, a jungle, Pacific Ocean, even climbing mountains. They found Christ everywhere! Our best friend and Saviour! More imagination followed in the 1998 program: A journey to the Holy Land, where the participants visited a carpenter's shop, using a hammer, a market in Jerusalem and a synagogue, as well as Mary and Martha in their home. They learned that all they need is faith the size of a mustard seed, and God will be an important friend for life. "Faith" became their "hit" song, and Joy Huettner's cookies sold well in the market! However, in the end, the introduction of the fee, however modest, led to fewer and fewer children participating, which ultimately resulted in the cancellation of the program at Tucker House. In recent years the BCBC summer program was conducted on BCBC's premises, where it benefitted from partial federal or provincial funding for one or two youth workers.

College and Careers. In 1995, Ruth Turle began a ministry to high school students, and in 1999 she recommended the establishment of a College and Careers group, thus creating a progression of ministry as the young people matured. Beginning in 1997, Charlotte Foster led a Bible class for college and careers ages, which focused on a study of comparative religion.[127] In 2001, her class focused on "Work-Serving God on the Job", a study that is part of the "Foundations for Christian Living Series", followed by other study themes.[128] The College and Careers group, which Ruth Turle had suggested, was eventually established in 2002-2004 by Jillian Zelmer and met on a weekly basis. During its first year, the group studied the book *The Purpose Driven Life*, by Rick Warren.[129]

In the early years, Pre-Teen and other Youth Group activities, including college and careers, were led by volunteers. In the fall of 2002, BCBC engaged Jillian Zelmer as part-time Minister of Youth, and since the summer of 2008, the Rev. Dean Noakes served as full-time pastor of Youth and Young Families. The global work undertaken by Jillian Zelmer and by Dean Noakes spanned both Teaching and Fellowship and was referenced in Chapter 5.

BILBERRY – *A Seed in Good Soil*

Chapter 9: Fellowship

Fellowship among Christians, known in the Greek New Testament as *koinonía*, describes the joy and bonds of oneness in the Lord, as referenced, among other passages, in Acts 2: 42 and 1. John 1:3. In the early church *fellowship* included the celebration of the *Love Feast*, or *Eucharist*, and for that reason it was originally intended to make BCBC's Fellowship Commission responsible, among other things, for the observance of the Lord's Supper. However, tradition prevailed, and responsibility for planning and leading the Lord's Supper became a *de facto* responsibility of the *Board of Deacons*.[130] That decision reduced "Fellowship" to hosting social events, however valuable and important these are.

In that context, although Adult Fellowship activities existed since 1986[131], the newly formed Fellowship Commission undertook a full Biblical study of the meaning of *fellowship* in 1988. In their first report[132] they stated:

> "From our study we began to realize the magnitude of fellowship as well as its potential. Our Fellowship should create a love for and unity with God and one another that cannot be broken. What an incredible opportunity for challenges as well as rewards! The possibilities are endless."

The same report continued:

> "Our initial endeavour as a committee was to look at all of the current programs and activities for fellowship at Bilberry Creek … Adult Fellowship… Teen Fellowship… Pre-teen Fellowship…Coffee Hour…Greeters at Worship… Host Family Program."[133]

The report also specified, as priorities for immediate attention, the Coffee Hour, Greeters at Worship and the Host Family Program.

Box 11. A 12 Kilometer Walk to Find a Church!

In the fall of 1991 Isaac Taweh Talla arrived in Canada from Cameroon while on assignment with the Cameroonian Embassy, where he worked as a driver for the embassy's diplomats. His wife Edith, and children Ginette, Addison and Lydie joined him in Canada in the spring of 1992. Isaac was a devout Christian who longed for Christian fellowship. Early one Sunday morning, shortly after his arrival, he set out on foot searching for a Baptist church. Over 12 km later, Isaac found Bilberry and soon became a part of our church family. In 1995, after his assignment had ended, he and his family returned to Anguissa, Yaoundé, Cameroon and to his church home at Faith Baptist Church. Addison is married and studying for the pastoral ministry at the Nigerian Baptist Theological Seminary in Ogbomosho, Nigeria.

Coffee Hour. With respect to the Coffee Hour, Cathy Collar had done that work single-handedly for several years. The Fellowship Commission proposed to involve more volunteers so as not to overburden her. Cathy, who is a professional dietician, agreed to prepare a *Procedure Sheet* for use by the volunteers with a view to ensuring that all necessary steps would be followed, and, particularly, that all hygienic requirements for a public food service would be met.

Greeters at Worship. The Greeters at Worship and Ushers had already been amalgamated. The Fellowship Commission suggested adding family members to act as Greeters and Ushers.

Host Family Program. The *Host Family Program* was envisioned as an expansion of the Greeters program, by including one designated family (adults and youth) per week to welcome worshippers as they arrive for a service, providing information, bulletins, etc, encouraging them to sign "welcome cards", and, when appropriate, to invite them to coffee or lunch and fellowship outings. Later, this program included an activity, organized by Helen Turle, known as "Guess who's Coming for Lunch".[134]

Although initially, the Fellowship Commission was meant to foster fellowship for all ages, the Commission proposed, ten years later, in 1998/99 that they concentrate more on "adult fellowship"[135] to help adults get to know one another better, particularly newer members. In that context a special event was a "Meet and Greet night", held in November of that year. While children and youth related fellowship activities were already an important component of the programs discussed under the Teaching Commission, the decision to focus the Commission's activity on adults may have been unfortunate in view of the significant work which had been done with Pre-Teens, Teens and College and Career groups, as discussed below. All fellowship-related programs are important activities for strengthening the fabric of the congregation. Many of these help members to bond and to build up each other's faith.

In actual experience, numerous fellowship activities have arisen, within or without the purview of the Fellowship Commission, that meet the social needs of the congregation. While most of these are internal to the church, some are inter-church events, such as the men's retreat at Camp Galilee,[136] which occurs annually, and the women's retreat at Camp Galilee which is sponsored by the Ottawa and Central

Associations of Baptist Churches. [137] Men were also involved in "Promise Keepers". [138] [139]

Other activities that are internal to BCBC and that have continued over time are the Men's Fellowship Breakfasts, Bilberry Baptist Women initiatives, a variety of adult fellowship activities and summer backyard fellowships.

Men's Fellowship. The Men's Fellowship Breakfasts were first reported in 1986[140], when they were held at the Normandy Restaurant; however, that venue ceased to exist when the restaurant closed in the summer of that year. Nevertheless, Men's Fellowship Breakfasts continued at unspecified other venues. [141] By 2006, the Men's Fellowship was described as "an excellent opportunity for men from both Bilberry and Église to connect with each other and with the community. Occasionally, their sons would also join them for breakfast." [142] Once per year the Men's Fellowship sponsored a "Women's Appreciation Breakfast" in May, close to Mother's Day. The same report indicates that the Men's Group has continued to support the outreach of the Capital City Mission by supplying knapsacks with various personal items. These were passed on to the Mission for distribution to both men and women who live on the streets of Ottawa. Customarily, the Men's Fellowship breakfasts include presentations by members or invited guests, such as, Alvin Gamble's presentation of slides and his talk on "The Churches in

Russia".[143] Over the years many other projects had been undertaken, such as the installation of a new floor in the new location of the Capital City Mission.

Bilberry Baptist Women. Fellowship meetings of women were recorded as early as 1986, led initially by Marguerite Hum and Alice Newsham, and later in the year by Darlene Tytula and Margaret Runacres. The purpose of the group was to allow ladies of Bilberry to get to know each other in a relaxed and informal way. The group's activities included study programs, one of which was a discussion based on a video tape series called "The Christian Home – A Woman's Perspective."[144] As early as 1990, an activity known as "Time Out" for women and children was offered on a weekly basis.[145] This activity was later led by Helen Turle at the home of Susan Moke under the name of "Moms and Tots".[146] Initially, the meetings occurred in members' homes, but were relocated to the church when the Phase I building became available.[147] In 2006, the Moms and Tots program was adopted by the Evangelism Commission, since it was a form of outreach to the community.[148] The 1997 activities included a winter retreat at the Baptist Church in Otter Lake, Quebec, at the invitation of its pastor Julie Ann Morton.[149]

Since 2001, the women's fellowship became known as *Bilberry Baptist Women*, which included plans for setting up an executive committee.[150] This change coincided with Lisee Kiar becoming the

BCBC liaison person with *Baptist Women of Ontario and Quebec* (BWOQ). As part of the programming of *Bilberry Baptist Women*, the winter outings that began in Otter Lake were later continued at Tucker House.[151] References to annual Algonquin canoe trips appear as early as 2001.[152] August long weekend camping was reported as early as 2004.[153] Throughout the year weekly Bible studies were held[154], as well as an annual event known as "prayer walks through the church".[155] Other activities included an "intergenerational tea for women and girls", as well as participation in the Ottawa Spring Rally and the BWOQ convention.[156]

Adult Fellowship Activities. An Adult Fellowship group was reported as early as 1986. Events in that year included: a Valentine's party at the Hum's; bowling; volleyball with the young people; games night; a fondue supper; skating on the canal; and swimming at the Rochow's.[157] Activities in other years included: a video night "The Hiding Place" at the Zelmer's; a slide presentation on Cyprus at the Oickle's, which concluded with a celebration of Don Collar's birthday; a presentation by Austin Moss on his heart transplant; mini-golf;[158] Friendship Sunday to reach out to those who attended only seldomly or never before;[159] a visit to a sugar bush; tip-toeing through the tulips, followed by tea at Rockliffe Park; camping at Lac Philippe;[160] a sleigh ride; hiking at Mer Bleu;[161] as a fund raiser, a cottage and craft sale, which yielded a net profit of about $317;[162] together with Grace Presbyterian Church, a car rally;[163] potluck suppers; church picnics;

outings to MacKenzie King Estate;[164] occasional "Days out with the Pastor", where interested adults and the Pastor visited neighbouring locations of interest; Newcomers' Luncheon; Mother's Day celebration;[165] BBQ on the church deck and lawns with volleyball, croquet and just visiting, for which invitations had been sent to approximately 60 homes neighbouring the church.[166]

Backyard Fellowship. The backyard fellowships began in the summer of 1986. The first ones were hosted by the Collars, the Newshams and the Turles. Subsequently, they were hosted regularly in July and August. In May 1990, Council Minutes reported that Backyard Fellowships would "reconvene" from June to September 1990.[167] In one year, one such gathering was used for brainstorming on outreach options.

Fellowship Activities for Youth. Starting in 1986 extensive fellowship activities for youth were undertaken, which included: Cross country skiing with Cam and Chris McIntyre; bowling; a slave day; volleyball and mini-golf, where each event included a devotional and refreshments. Fall and winter activities under the leadership of Fred and Rene Weiss included: Horseback riding; a movie night "A Time to Run"; sleep-over at Tucker House; a tape by Mike Warnke; a Christmas banquet; tobogganing; and a games night and devotions at the Newsham's. In July the young people assisted a team from the Baptist Youth Corps to conduct a children's outreach ministry in Queenswood Heights, which was an excellent opportunity for fellowship, growing and learning.[168] In 1987 other new activities were undertaken, which include: Swimming and water slide; participation in first summer Youth Campout at Lac Philippe; movies ("The Hiding Place", "A Thief in the Night", and "Distant Thunder"); and the presentation of a drama during the Christmas season entitled "Humbug".[169] Activities in 1988 included: Bowling; a Grease Night; Mystery Nights; a Scavenger Hunt; with Bromley Baptist Church Youth, a "Banana and Dog Night" and a "Wake Over" at Tucker House; a "Missing Person" event at a local mall; skating on the Canal; Fun Day in Kanata, followed by a rally led by a Team from the *Baptist Leadership Education Center* (BLEC); a youth retreat at Camp Iwah; a fall McBanquet at Bromley Road Baptist Church; and participation by some youths in various other Association events sponsored by OTTABY.[170] In 1988, the church received a request from the young people to set up a fund for less fortunate youth to attend special functions. David Oickle and Carl Sears would identify individuals on a case by case basis, keeping a confidential record.[171] In 1989, BCBC youth met monthly with youth from Pinegrove Christian Fellowship, Grace Presbyterian, and Redeemer Alliance for an evening of fellowship and fun, calling themselves the "FAB 4". On a larger basis, the *Orleans Youth Ministries* included young people from seven churches that often attracted about 100 participants, many of whom were unchurched.[172] In 1997-1998, special events included swimming in Foster's pool and involvement in Billy Graham events (Go Mad youth night), as reported by Ruth Turle.[173] In the early years the youth program was offered by volunteers, such as Ruth Turle, [174] Jeff Parke[175], as well as by Julie and Amanda, Kim Jens, Trisha Jennings and Sharon O'Brien. In 2001, Don Collar reported that "this year has been a year for 'rebuilding' our youth ministry. I have worked along side Jeff Parke each week in providing adult leadership to the group." Dawn McCleave ensured that the GAP was included in the BCBC website.[176]

Fellowship Activities for Pre-Teens. The Pre-Teen Group (ages 9-12) was organized in September 1987 by Mary Wehrle and Helen Turle under the direction of Pastor Don Collar. In their words:

> "The purpose of this group is to provide twice monthly an opportunity for fellowship with Christian youngsters of the same age. During their time together the values of friendship,

sharing and Christian attitudes to one another are stressed. It is hoped that the Pre-Teen group will recognize this church event as a social meeting point, and as they grow into being teenagers and adults, this initial bond with the church and the Lord will be strengthened.

Because of the ages of the Pre-Teens their time together is divided between an activity and a time of worship and learning about their Lord. Some of the fall activities included: bowling, swimming, crafts, games night, collective birthday party and a progressive supper."[177]

By 1989 the Pre-Teens group had grown to 18-20 and included children from outside BCBC. New activities included: Mini golf, singing carols to seniors at Laurier Manor, curling, video night, gym night with the Cornerstone Church, and an India night with John and Martha Easter, missionaries of the *Canadian Baptist Overseas Mission Board*.[178]

In 1990, Cathy and Don Collar gave leadership to this group. Unique activities that year included a visit by the Cheveldayoff's, then missionaries to Bolivia, as well as a sleep-over at the end of the yearly program.[179] While Cathy and Don were still giving leadership to this group in 1992-1993, Char and Stew Radford assisted in supervising this group. All four continued doing so in 1994.[180] A special event in

---

Box 12. A Pre-Teen and Junior High Trip to Brownsburg, Québec, led by Bonnie Maitland, Pre-Teen Leader.

Our highlight was our trip to Brownsburg, Québec. We checked into the empty house where I grew up, chose our sleeping spots, and quickly got back into the cars and headed to the "real" country (gravel roads) where friends greeted us and treated us to a taffy party – all we could eat! The Junior Highs, who joined us that weekend were thrilled to be there as well. After a tour and explanation of maple syrup making, some of us got to help make the final batch of syrup for the year. We said goodbye and went back to Brownsburg, got ready for bed and then made mini pizzas for a midnight snack. We, the leaders, played Trivial Pursuit until the last of the 13 went to sleep at 3 a.m. Sunday morning we practised our song, had breakfast, got ready for church (11 a.m.) and still had an hour to spare. The children sang "Trust in the Lord with Your H-E-A-R-T", to the great delight of the congregation at Maple Avenue Baptist Church, and Janice and I sang in a trio with the pastor, Daryl Levy. After the service we had a pizza party in the church basement. After clean-up, we parted, and some headed home, while my group continued to Lachute to visit with my Mom and other senior residents. On our way home, we stopped and watched, as the Canada Geese landed in the field next to the highway.

The children saw and experienced the wonder of God all around them that weekend. They talked about it all the way home (one fell asleep!). Bonnie Maitland

---

1996 was a trip to Brownsburg, Quebec, organized by Bonnie Maitland [181] (see Box 12). As of October 4, 2002, the Pre-Teen work was executed by Jillian Zelmer as part of her role as Minister of Youth.[182]

Over the years, a host of midweek fellowship groups arose to respond to the unique needs of the congregation.

To foster interaction among church families, a Church Pictorial Directory was produced in the fall of 1997.[183]

Chapter 10: Service

Service was the original function of "deacons", *diakonía* in the Greek New Testament, as described in Acts 6: 1-4, where the Early Church was so absorbed in worship, preaching, teaching and fellowship that they forgot the needs of hungry widows. Thus "deacons" were appointed to provide for the physical needs of the less fortunate.

The care for the less fortunate is still the controlling feature of the service ministry, whether led by the Service Commission, or not. At BCBC, the service ministry falls into four broad administrative categories: (1) Services delivered with BCBC participation through community organizations; (2) direct BCBC service programs; (3) collaboration of the Service Commission with other BCBC Commissions; and (4) BCBC service ministries in collaboration with other churches.

BCBC Service Ministry Through Community Organizations

Services delivered with BCBC participation through community organizations involved: The *Community Resource Centre* (CRC)[184]; the *Gloucester Emergency Food Cupboard*; the *Union Mission*; the *Salvation Army*; the *Miriam Centre* and the Matthew 2535 Network[185], of which BCBC is a member, by vote of Council.

In 1991, as part of the Angel Tree project, 70 angels were made, of which approximately 65 angel tree gifts were picked up and taken to the *Community Resource Centre*, where the staff was extremely overwhelmed and thankful. Unfortunately, in future, gifts cannot be wrapped, since that had been misused.[186] The congregation has also been saving coupons which were given to the CRC so that they could cash them in for food for the needy.[187] In its annual meeting, on May 28, 1992, in recognition of BCBC's support, the CRC presented BCBC with its *Community Service Certificate*. The Angel Tree project continued throughout the years, although with some variation. For instance in 2002, the Angel Tree at Christmas provided a gift or two for needy BCBC families, with the remainder going to a "toy mountain" to be distributed in the community generally.[188]

The *Gloucester Emergency Food Cupboard* opened its doors on January 18, 1989, and, from the very beginning, Don Collar served on its Board of Directors [189]. Members of the congregation volunteered at *Gloucester Emergency Food Cupboard* in 1996/97[190], and again in 1997/98, including young people.[191] Don Collar, then Chairman of the Board of Directors, reported in 1994 that unfortunately, there is a growing need for this service among our community's working poor. In 1993, the cupboard provided food for nearly 17,000 people. The food distributed was worth $17 per person." [192] In October 2000, BCBC held a "berry drive" and contributed 50% of the profit to a local food bank.[193]

BCBC supported the *Union Mission* with food and clothing. For a single meal on January 18, 1992, the Mission expected between 300 and 400 people who were living on the streets to come for dinner.[194] Bev Chomcey's account in Box 13 describes the close bonds and mutual blessings between the servers and the people served.[195] The work at the Union Mission involves more than food and clothing; it is also conversation, sometimes over games, showing a movie or helping them wrap gifts.[196] Support of the *Salvation Army* is mostly in the form of used, but good, clothing. As part of the food and clothing drive at BCBC in February 1992, women's and children's clothing was made available to the *Miriam Centre*,[197] and in 1994, a small amount for the support for the *Miriam Centre* was included in the BCBC budget.[198] BCBC also participated in Community Relief Funds, as in the case of a gas line explosion in the neighbourhood.[199]

> **Box 13: Union Mission. An Excerpt by Bev Chomcey.**
> "There was a lot that has happened at the Union Mission this past year and we'll start with every third Saturday of every month, [when] we serve a nice dinner to the homeless. We provide the desserts and the Union Mission provides the meals. But the guys, and now unfortunately a few women and children, really enjoy sitting down and being served, as it is a real treat. We have had the opportunity to get to know quite a few of the men that are there and they especially look forward to our coming each month. In fact, if we aren't there they ask us why we didn't come or where is so and so. I can honestly say we look forward to going there because God is really working there, both by the staff and men and all the volunteers. It is such a wonderful feeling to know that God's love is there."

Direct BCBC Service Programs

The direct BCBC service programs include the operation of a self-help church-based food cupboard for needy families, as well as targeted prepared meal support for persons during bereavement, short-term illness, other incapacitation or difficult times.[200] The Commission requested church members to inform them of illness or special needs so that they can respond either for the provision of meals, transportation or other needs[201]. In 1990, food was collected from church families on Communion Sundays, and given to the Food Cupboard; however, that program stopped because of lack of interest. Also in 1990, mittens, socks, hats and snowsuits were collected and presented to the *Snowsuit Fund*. During the same year cans were distributed to church families to collect change. That resulted in about $185, half of which collected by the Sunday School, which was contributed to the Food Cupboard.[202] The first food cupboard to store and display food items was established in 1995/96.[203] The current cupboard is a Christmas gift of Don and Cathy Collar.[204] The *Food Hamper Program* involves the preparation of food hampers at Christmas, Easter and Thanksgiving.[205] Throughout the years, a *Benevolent Fund* was administered by the Board of Deacons. BCBC also responds to emergencies spontaneously.

Rehabilitation under the Community Service Order. A service ministry of a different kind is the supervision of offenders doing work under *Community Service Orders*. An example of evidence of the impact of this ministry is that in 1999, a previous CSO worker donated his truck to transport the platforms to the church which Don and Cathy Collar had purchased from Eaton's.[206] In 2001, the pastor reported that he had supervised eight "Community Service Volunteers" doing many hours of janitorial work, whose work has to be monitored and reported. In particular, he pointed out that:

> "I am grateful for the number of occasions God has provided for me to speak to the workers about their concerns and the place Christ could have in their lives. Steve, one of the workers, considers Bilberry to be 'his church'. He has had many meaningful "religious" talks with Bonnie Maitland while he had been at Bilberry doing his service hours. He is grateful for Bilberry's prayers on his behalf."[207]

Refugee Support. Since refugee support is an aspect of the care for the less fortunate, it is clearly a form of *service ministry*, but in the past such an activity was not administered by BCBC's *Service Commission*. Instead, Council guided refugee support on an ad hoc basis. At one point, an unknown source produced an undated document entitled *Guidelines for Sponsorship of Refugee*[208] which was submitted to Council for consideration prior to the upcoming annual budget meeting. It is likely that this document was prepared with a view to sponsoring Mohamud Issa. This document called for the definition of

Terms of Reference, Expectations of the Applicant, Definition of the Process, and Recommendations.

The earliest reference to refugee support by BCBC goes back to 1987, when Dr. Richard Coffin of the Baptist Federation of Canada referred a refugee claimant to the Pastor, who, in response, provided assistance through the *Benevolence Fund*.[209]

The 1989 Annual Report, indicates that "the church family has rallied around John and Erica Dodis during a very difficult time in their life."[210] The same Annual Report indicated that the most difficult experience of the Dodis family was the death of their son.[211] The support to the Dodis family included writing a letter to the *Department of Employment and Immigration*, requesting that a work permit be issued to John.[212] Both John and Erica Dodis were baptized at BCBC in 1990.[213]

The 1989 Annual Report also mentions that "Bilberry agreed to act as sponsor for a Chinese gentleman, whose wife is desperately seeking to bring him into Canada". At the May 1990 Council meeting, "Carl Sears moved that BCBC sponsor a Chinese individual [presumably the same person] for a student visa and that his name be used as guarantor", while BCBC and the *New Wine Church* would be liable for actual support. Council approved the motion.[214]

Eleven years later, in 2001, BCBC succeeded in sponsoring Mohamud Issa, a refugee from Somalia. The Challenger, introducing "Frequently Asked Questions", fittingly quoted Matthew 25:38: "When, Lord, did we see you a stranger and welcome you in our homes or naked and clothe you?"[215]

A background note on his sponsorship included the following:

> "During the civil war in Somalia, when Mohamud was only 18 years old, his father and brother were killed. He escaped to Kenya, but lost contact with his mother [from] whom he has not heard for 10 years. He does not even know whether she is still alive. In Kenya, Mohamud survived by his wits as a refugee, refusing to take drugs – although some other refugees were – and refusing to steal."[216]

The same background note explains that churches and individuals made donations to the Sharing Way through the Baptist Refugee Committee, on which BCBC, as steward of that money, could draw to meet the required $7,000 annual support budget. As a minor variation, the BCBC report of the Annual Program meeting on June 16, 2001 indicates that the Sharing Way contributed only $6,000 and that BCBC held $1,000 in reserve.[217] The $7,000 amount covered a one bedroom rental unit (about $350 per month), food and sundries (about $250 per month) and a bus pass ($65 per month). The Salvation Army helped with clothing for the fall and winter, and BCBC was working with a local thrift shop for remaining items. BCBC also helped Mohamud to obtain a social insurance number and an OHIP card.

Upon Mohamud's arrival, Pastor Don Collar, Winston Caesar and Bob Foster met him at the airport. For two weeks he stayed at the International Youth Hostel. It so happened that a Christian couple in Orleans was looking for a house sitter for two months during the summer and were happy to help.[218]

Subsequently, housing arrangements were made with Winston Caesar. This meant that Mohamud, a Muslim, experienced Christian love on a daily basis. He also met other BCBC members at a backyard fellowship at the Fosters and at some other BCBC functions. Nevertheless, to the church's credit, its outpouring of Christian love was pure and not subject to any form of religious coercion.

Years later, in 2006, Mohamud wrote to the church from Calgary where he was then working in a meat processing plant:

> "...I can not forget how the members of Bilberry Creek Baptist Church helped me when I was in Ottawa. I was very grateful for your help and that of Winston, Bob Foster and his wife, and Cathy...."[219]

In the same letter, Mohamud mentioned that after many years he had made contact with his mother in Somalia and was hoping to make arrangements for bringing her to Canada.

Collaboration with Other BCBC Commissions.

The Service Commission collaborated with the Fellowship Commission in the hosting of an annual "Meet and Greet Dinner" for newcomers, where the Pastoral Care group provided dessert and coffee.[220]

BCBC Service Ministry in Collaboration with Other Churches

The prime example of BCBC service ministry in collaboration with other churches is the *Community Employment Action Program* (CEAP), which BCBC planned beginning in February 1995[221], and initiated in collaboration with four other churches in the Orleans area, on September 11, 1995 [222]. The other churches were *St. Helen's Anglican Church, Divine Infant Catholic Church, Orleans United Church* and *Queenswood United Church*. CEAP initially involved 48 volunteer staff from the five churches. At a later time *Paroisse St-Joseph* (i.e. St. Joseph's Parish) became involved through *Le Centre d'alphabetisation "Le Trésor des Mots"* [223] to serve the French speaking population. St. Joseph's Parish also accepted responsibility, in November 1996, for administering CEAP finances.[224]

This ministry was in response to the severe reduction of employment in the federal public service in the mid-1990s. An article in the *Ottawa Citizen* demonstrates the magnitude of need at that time, comparing the list of 2010 jobless public servants with the much higher job loss in the mid 1990s (i.e. at the time when CEAP was established), when "up to 50,000 jobs were wiped off the payroll".[225] Another article in the *Ottawa Citizen*, dated February 13, 1996, and entitled "No work, no hope: 40,000 in region give up job search",[226] reported that "Ottawa-Hull is harder hit by hidden unemployment than virtually any other major city in the country."

In October 1995, *The Ottawa Times* published an article, entitled: "Churches play key role in business sector: Local Churches Unite to Help Unemployed Back on their Feet",[227] and the *Cumberland Communiqué* published an article and contact data in October 1995.[228]

On January 13, 1996 Bob Harvey, of the *Ottawa Citizen* published an article entitled "Compassion moves churches to job-training".[229] Bob Harvey's article was also published in *The Edmonton Journal*[230], *The Calgary Herald*[231], *The Sudbury Star*,[232] *The Toronto Star*,[233] the latter calling it a "'Grand concept' [that] is role model for all communities." Apparently, in response to early media releases, *CBC Radio Morningside* requested background information.[234]

The Editor of the *Orleans Weekly Journal* reported on the reach and impact of CEAP, as quoted in Box 14, calling it a success story.

Box 14. Community Employment Action Program.
Article: "Take pride in success of Employment Action Program", by Michael
Curren, Editor of the *Orleans Weekly Journal* (February 3, 1996, page 6).

"It's a success story that all of us should applaud but too few of us
know about. It's being talked about across the country and receiving
press coverage in newspapers from Halifax to Calgary as well as a
television coverage in Vancouver.

What could be attracting so much attention? The rekindled spirit of the
Ottawa Senators or the opening of the Palladium? No, but it's just as
miraculous. Is it the Prime Minister's Unity Plan? No, this program is
saleable, and unlike Mr. Chretien's, is helping put people back to
work.

We're talking about the Community Employment Action Program.
The initiative was launched last September, when five Orléans
churches – Bilberry Creek Baptist, Divine Infant Catholic, St. Helen's
Anglican, Queenswood United and Orléans United – pulled together to
explore what could be done to support people suffering from job loss.

CEAP was created as a church sponsored program run by volunteers to
respond to people in crisis, regardless of religious denomination. Free
support is available to help people cope with the spiritual and
emotional stresses of unemployment. What is truly innovative is the
practical manner in which the CEAP helps people pinpoint opening.

Here's how it works. After attending seminars about subjects such as
resume preparation, participants can submit information so that a
databank of skills is compiled. The parishioners from the five churches
(virtually thousands of people) act as the eyes and ears of the
unemployed. For example, if an employed parishioner hears of a
resignation in their office, they phone CEAP and inform it of a
possible job opening. Once the job requirements are ascertained, the
CEAP swings into action, finding a suitably trained person and
providing him or her with a contact at the business.

The program recognizes that only one in five job opportunities is advertised in newspaper and other media. The remaining jobs are publicized through word of mouth. What could be more practical? What a terrific opportunity for these community institutions to demonstrate they have not lost relevance to life in the '90s. The CEAP initiative confirmed the churches are in tune with a serious crisis for many in our community.

Five months after its inception, the idea has spread across Ottawa-Carleton, across the province and even across the country. Credit for the program must go to people like Gunter Rochow of Bilberry Baptist Church and the hundreds of volunteers who provide job leads. These people are now realizing the pleasure of success, and indeed, it's richly deserved."

Laurie McBurney, on the *Orleans Weekly Journal*[235] staff added:

"A recent feature article about CEAP in a local newspaper has apparently intrigued media across the country. Rochow appeared on a CBC-TV Vancouver news program that was broadcast throughout the western provinces. The article was also published in the Toronto Star, and Rochow received calls from Sudbury, the North Bay social services department, Halifax and Dartmouth."

The same article quotes Gunter Rochow as saying:

"Right now we are faced with a crisis situation (unemployment) that requires intervention. Once the crisis is over, we will discontinue the program. We do not want to duplicate existing services."

Vision TV filmed a CEAP documentary[236] on Sunday, February 25 and Monday, February 26, 1996, which was televised later in the spring. On Canada Day 1996, *MacLean's Magazine* published an article entitled "The Community Employment Action Program – its beginnings and workings".[237] Other press coverage included: Kanata Kourier Standard.[238]

From its cradle in Orleans, active programs were set up in Ottawa: *Emmanuel United Church* on Smyth Road; in the west end by a group of churches headed by *Bethany Baptist Church*; and in centre town by *St. George's Anglican Church.*[239] Reinhilde and Gunter Rochow were also invited to the Ottawa Mennonite Church on November 26, 1995 to make a presentation on CEAP to their adult Sunday School. Also, a church in Brantford, Ontario, asked Reinhilde and Gunter to visit them to help plan for a similar service.

As for the Orleans churches, each hosted CEAP for one evening per week, Mondays to Fridays. With regard to BCBC's continuing involvement, Betty and Campbell Stephens wrote in the Easter 1996 Challenger:

> "We'd like to stress the importance of the entire congregation 'pulling together' to assist us with 'Job leads'. Even a 'small thing' --- like keeping your eyes open to 'Help Wanted' signs in a store window, as you are shopping. We have an enthusiastic 'Group' from our Church, working on various jobs

for this 'Program'. Our 'Counsellors are Rev. Rob Campbell, Carol Avery and Campbell Stephens. Daytime Telephone Receptionist is Helen Turle. Evening Receptionists are Bing Hum, Virginia Maloney, Charlotte Foster, Shirley Shearer and Betty Stephens. We could use one more evening Receptionist, if anyone could volunteer one evening every few weeks... Due to the 'Report' given by Gunter Rochow, to the 'Cumberland Council', we were given a 'grant' for extra 'phone – lines'."[240]

On January 6, 1996, Gunter Rochow was the guest speaker at a meeting of the *Rotary Club*,[241] to present CEAP.

Chapter 11: Working with Other Churches

From the beginning, BCBC perceived itself to be only one expression of the larger Body of Christ. This is reflected in the extensive linkages and collaboration with other churches in pursuit of its ministry, both within the Baptist tradition and beyond.

Within the family of Baptist Churches, BCBC is linked to the *Ottawa Association of Baptist Churches* (OABC), the *Canadian Baptists of Ontario and Quebec* (CBOQ), as well as *Canadian Baptist Ministries* (CBM). The latter is the organization that delivers Christian witness and service primarily abroad. However, in the 1990s it also sponsored a *Public Affairs Committee*, of which Gunter Rochow was a member, which addressed subjects such as: Family issues (including divorce, aging, person abuse); social mores (gambling/lotteries, substance abuse, pornography, abortion, bio-ethics, euthanasia, sexual orientation); national issues (Constitutional issues, human rights, use of Sunday, justice and correction, environment, poverty, housing, employment, health and welfare, group rights, unity and equality); and international issues (human rights, peace, and refugees).

BCBC was heavily involved with the *Ottawa Association of Baptist Churches* (OABC) in many ways, by sending its delegates to annual functions and participating in Good Friday services at *First Baptist Church*, where Don Collar also took his turn preaching. Over the years,

Don executed several OABC leadership functions, including the role of Moderator in 1997-1998. In that role he was involved, among other things, in planting the new Longfields Baptist Church. In 2003-2004, Don served on the Association's *Nurture Committee*, which sponsored seminars on the Old and New Testaments, the latter at BCBC.

BCBC also sent delegates to annual functions of CBOQ and served on its boards, committees and in other ways. For example, Don Collar was a member of CBOQ's *By-Law Committee* and Betty Stephens was Vice-President of the *Baptist Women's and Missionary Association* from 1990 to 1992. Delegates to CBOQ included Austin and Mary Moss, Campbell and Betty Stephens, Kim and Paul Barriault, Elaine and Art Eckert, and Richard and Helen Turle. As referenced in Chapter 7, several BCBC members also provided supply preaching in other churches.

For worship and instructional materials, BCBC drew, among others, on resources prepared by both the *Canadian Council of Churches* and the *Evangelical Fellowship of Canada*. Don Collar collaborated with the Rev. Gordon Kouwenberg from Grace Presbyterian Church in organizing a Family Enrichment Seminar and a seminar entitled "Romance and Sex".

The BCBC young people participated city-wide in a large number of interdenominational events, including "Orleans Youth Ministries", which involved seven area churches. The bi-monthly meetings attracted about 100 participants in each event, many of whom were unchurched.

As discussed in Chapter 10 on *Service*, in the Orleans area, following the large scale downsizing in the federal public service, BCBC collaborated as a lead church with several area churches in the *Community Employment Action Program* (CEAP), which included Orleans United and Queenswood United Churches, St. Helen's Anglican and Divine Infant Roman Catholic Church. Later other churches joined as well, including St. Joseph's Roman Catholic Church.

BILBERRY – *A Seed in Good Soil*

PART III: REFLECTION AND OUTLOOK

Chapter 12: What Does it all Mean?

In Parts I and II we reviewed the planning for ministry and BCBC's ministry itself. In Part III we are drawing some conclusions about the church's experience in terms of its impact on the church members and adherents, as well as on the community.

How Healthy is the Church?

In 2000, the *Baptist Convention of Ontario and Quebec* (BCOQ), now known as *Canadian Baptists of Ontario and Quebec* (CBOQ), issued *A Framework for Action (2000)*[242], a document for discussion and input that was to be presented to the BCOQ Assembly in the same year. The Framework identified eight characteristics of a healthy church. These serve as indicators to help us interpret the significance of the many activities which BCBC undertook during its first 25 years, and they can also serve as indictors of the church's health during future years.

The eight characteristics are: (1) Empowering leadership assists Christians to attain their spiritual potential; (2) gift-oriented ministry encourages Christians to serve in their areas of giftedness; (3) Passionate spirituality engages a clear witness of faith; (4) functional structures improve the organization of the church; (5) inspiring worship services celebrate the presence of the Holy Spirit, which is felt in the service; (6) holistic small groups move beyond discussion of

Bible passages to apply the message to daily life; (7) need-oriented evangelism focuses evangelistic efforts on the questions and needs of non-Christians; and (8) loving relationships enable people to experience authentic Christian love.[243]

In reviewing these eight characteristics, it is noteworthy that they all focus on "outcomes" of ministry, not just on "activities" or "outputs". Nevertheless, as we look at the general health of the church in terms of outcomes, it is also appropriate to include a look at the overall numbers, since these are a proxy for the church's health in general.

Empowering Leadership *"Empowering leadership assists Christians to attain their spiritual potential."*

The hallmark of Don Collar's ministry was one of equipping and empowering others. The Pastoral Care team was an example of lay persons reaching out to the congregation in close collaboration with the pastor. Normally the members of the Pastoral Care team had received specific training for that role. Nevertheless, not all who were trained in pastoral care belonged to the formal Pastoral Care team, but rather exercised that function freely in their relation with others. It may be a brother or sister in the next chair who felt the caring embrace. While one of the originally intended roles of the Pastoral Care team was to support the pastor with visitation on the basis of alphabetically assigned members and adherents, that proved to be difficult to execute. In several families, especially those where husband and wife were working, routine visits were on occasion not considered to be welcome; rather, the notion was frequently expressed "we will call you when we need you". As an alternative to visitation, the option of maintaining occasional telephone contacts had been considered.

The original five (and later six) Commissions ministered in their respective areas, albeit within the constraints of BCBC's Constitution and policies. While the Commissions provided helpful ministry-oriented structures, and while there was some room for improvement in terms of inter-relationships, coherence and the integration of some emerging activities, there was no doubt that all leaders felt empowered and displayed their commitment to the ministry that had been entrusted to them.

By way of example, Sharon Cavey involved those young people in Junior Church who were willing to make the necessary commitment. Thus, members of the *College and Careers Group* took on more and more responsibilities, including participation in the summer program. Also Bonnie Maitland and Janice Rochow fostered the musical skills of children with a view of ultimately enabling them to participate in the regular church band.

Gift-Oriented Ministry

"Gift-oriented ministry encourages Christians to serve in their areas of giftedness."

Don Collar's commitment to his pastoral, chaplaincy and community roles, as well as his skills as a facilitator not only displayed his own gift-oriented ministry, but it encouraged others to do likewise.

While the members of the Pastoral Care team received special training, they were mainly driven by their passion to be pastoral care givers. Carmen Paul, who had throughout her life dedicated much of her time to prayer, rallied others who shared similar concerns.

Douglas Rochow and other writers of Christian music, such as Barry Francis, enriched BCBC's repertoire for worship. Bonnie Maitland, much beyond her role in *Music Alive*, encouraged community service workers. Bob Zelmer used his special skills in site planning. Carl Sears applied his accounting skills as Treasurer. Bob Foster's administrative skills made him an effective Moderator of Council. Art Eckert's business skills were a rich resource for his role as trustee. The trustees as a group looked out for BCBC's financial health by investigating and securing savings on insurance premiums. Gunter Rochow made the first attempts while serving as Trustee on the *Carleton Board of Education* to have the need for School Board Chaplaincy considered. Helen Turle fostered opportunities for newcomers to meet members of the congregation. BCBC's architect for Phase I, Harry Ala-Kantti, was overjoyed seeing that children painted as high as they could reach, only to let their parents and other adults take over when a higher reach was required. The list could go on and on of people who volunteered when a need arose and their response to the extent that they were able to be helpful.

Passionate Spirituality
"Passionate spirituality engages a clear witness of faith."

At BCBC passionate spirituality was expressed in many forms, due in part to the culturally diverse and multi-generational make-up of the congregation, but in all its diversity, there was no doubt about the clarity of the witness of faith of the members of the congregation. Many members and adherents were passionate about studying the Bible, which led them to participate in Bible studies and to take notes during preaching. Jun Zhang left no doubt about the evidence of physical healing (Box 5). Bonnie Maitland bubbled over when relating her faith to the community service workers or when working with pre-teens. With the expansion of Bits and Bytes, many people requested prayer and reported on answers to prayer. Others evidenced their spirituality in the singing of traditional hymns or in modern Christian songs.

Functional Structures

"Functional structures improve the organization of the church."

To foster functional structures, BCBC chose to have a *Covenant*; it does not have a *Statement of Faith*. It established ministry-oriented *Commissions*, and not secular structures, and it pursued responsible approaches to finance.

Statement of Faith versus Covenant. When BCBC was organized, its members did not perceive the need for a *Statement of Faith*, which normally sets boundaries that tend to *exclude* people. Instead of such a Statement, BCBC developed a *Covenant*, which is designed to *include* fellow Christians who commit themselves to share their gifts, time and resources in serving their Lord through a local congregation. In the case of BCBC that decision made it possible to *include* in the fellowship many faithful Christians of diverse backgrounds.

Commissions. The concept of Commissions was defined at the very beginning of BCBC's life in the belief that biblical structures of ministry are more important for the growth of a healthy church than secular organizational patterns. Nevertheless, it was soon recognized that this innovative approach also entailed some difficulties in that it conflicted with some traditional organizational models in Baptist churches and that it did not easily integrate all ministry practices that arose over time. Yet, the congregation continued to work through

Commissions, because they were not aware of a better model. In general, the Commissions were introduced in accordance with the congregation's priorities and perceived strengths and weaknesses of the members interested in serving on the Commissions.

The *Worship Commission*, which was intended to foster both public and private worship, concentrated on public worship. This Commission fulfilled an exceedingly important function in strengthening the unity of the church through well integrated inter-generational worship by blending traditional hymns with more modern musical styles. Nevertheless, this blending was no easy exercise, since modern music is often highly syncopated to which older members are usually not accustomed.

Also, the Commission ensured that worship fully engaged the congregation by encouraging regular participatory singing complemented by some solo or group performance.

In concept, the *Preaching, Mission and Evangelism Commission*, was intended to focus on the biblical concept of announcing the *kerygma*, i.e. the Good News, at home and abroad. However, in practice this Commission never formally addressed the "preaching" component. The original intent was to foster preaching not only by the pastor in BCBC's Sunday services, but to encourage a preaching culture among qualified members which would extend the reach of the congregation beyond its walls into other congregations on a supply basis, as well as into nursing homes, other institutions and ultimately into emerging new congregations. In practice, the oversight of pastoral preaching on Sundays became a responsibility of the Deacons. While preaching outside BCBC occurred to a considerable extent, it was viewed as an ad hoc desirable activity of individual members and not as an intentional thrust of the home church.

The remaining elements of the *Preaching, Mission and Evangelism Commission*, i.e. Mission and Evangelism, ultimately were split in two, since its members who were committed to mission abroad did not feel to be capable of promoting as well evangelism at home. Consequently, that Commission became known simply as *Mission Commission*. However, ultimately, when the need was identified to undertake evangelism at home, a new *Commission on Evangelism* was established.

The *Teaching Commission* was intended to be modelled on Jesus' ministry of teaching, drawing on a large range of opportunities for lifelong learning. In practice, this "Commission" focused initially on the Sunday School, and only over time did it begin to address its broader mandate, and, even at that, much remains to be done to achieve its full mandate. The reason for focusing on the Sunday School is obvious: There were only a few volunteers available, and the Sunday School was the top priority for this Commission.

The *Fellowship Commission* was meant to promote the biblical concept of *koinonía*, i.e. of joy of communion with the Lord and among believers. In biblical terms that included the planning for, and delivery of, the love feast, Eucharist or Lord's Supper. In practice, this commission did not pursue the opportunity of becoming a vibrant in-depth organ to promote fellowship in the deepest sense, and instead it limited itself to promoting social events, however important, and that mostly among adults. The administration of the Lord's Supper, following tradition among Baptists, became a responsibility of the Deacons in collaboration with the Worship Commission. Nevertheless, the Fellowship Commission, as an instrument for planning social events has done very valuable work in response to congregational needs.

Responsible Finance. In terms of finance, BCBC avoided grandiose expenditures which might have stifled the congregation due to unnecessary monetary obligations. Instead, thanks, in part, to its architect, Harry Ala-Kantti, BCBC opted for a simple Phase I structure along with plug-in – plug-out portables which entailed an affordable financial commitment. The same thinking prevailed during the planning for Phase II expansion. The *Partnership of Equals* in the co-location of the two congregations offering ministries in English and French, is an excellent example of how two compatible organizations can plan and work in one cost-effective facility. Following a recommendation from CBOQ, and thanks to the advice of BCBC's lawyer, Mr. Les Bunning, risks were minimized through *incorporation* of the church. As for summer help, the church worked prudently with partial support from *Ontario Works* and *Human Resources and Skills Development Canada* (HRSDC).

Inspiring Worship

"Inspiring worship services celebrate the presence of the Holy Spirit, which is felt in the service."

BCBC lived its fundamental objective of *glorifying God*. Again, the form of worship varied somewhat among worship leaders and pastors responsible for particular services. Almost invariably, a worship service ended with an *invitation to prayer*. The fact that many people came forward was a sign that they were touched by the message and the worship experience. The evidence that worship inspired, is that people regularly recommitted their lives or chose faith in Christ for the first time.

Towards the end of BCBC's first twenty-five years, Gunter Rochow and Richard Turle, with the extensive support of Reinhilde and Waldo Rochow, assembled and edited a collection of twenty-five of Don Collars sermons which were judged to have been especially inspiring. These were published and presented to him on the occasion of his personal twenty-fifth anniversary as pastor at BCBC in the spring of

2010, under the title of: *The Word – In celebration of 25 years of ministry at Bilberry Creek Baptist Church.*[244]

As already discussed in the context of the Worship Commission, BCBC has successfully shaped and practised intergenerational worship, by blending traditional hymns with modern musical expressions. In blending the musical styles, BCBC is not responding to a popularity contest, but rather to the varying needs of ministry.

Inspiring worship is also enhanced by maintaining an uninterrupted flow within the worship experience. This is done by making all necessary announcements at the beginning of the service. The offering is part of the worship as an expression of self-giving to God. As such, it is not just a collection. While it has often been attempted to foster inspiring worship by meditating before the service and maintaining silence before and after, this has generally not been successful, in part because of another noble competing goal, that of greeting and welcoming one another.

Need-oriented Evangelism

"Need-oriented evangelism focuses evangelistic efforts on the questions and needs of non-Christians."

In the area of evangelism, BCBC had offered a mix of supply and demand-driven approaches. On the supply side, evangelism was offered to others by traditional means whether they sensed a need for it or not, through such approaches as the door-to-door contacts in the community, the Jesus video, the Parade of Lights and the Canada Day activities, where the participants reached out to people at large who do not have a regular involvement in a Christian church.

Need-oriented evangelism requires a thorough understanding of the community and the needs of people. Such evangelism involves building relationships and responding to people's needs from a Christian perspective. The prime example at BCBC of demand driven need-oriented evangelism was the prison ministry, which reached mostly unchurched people. It was demand driven, since the access to Alpha program sessions was numerically limited for security reasons, and participants had to request permission to participate.

Within the congregation the need for commitment to Christ was ever present in Sunday services, Sunday School and weekday events. Over and above that, since establishing the Evangelism Commission, BCBC had been strengthening its outreach through needs-oriented evangelism. Nevertheless, while the congregation was well on its way to becoming a healthy church in the area of evangelism, this remains to be a form of ministry where there is room for extensive improvement.

Holistic Small Groups

"Holistic small groups move beyond discussion of Bible passages to apply the message to daily life."

Throughout its history BCBC has given strong evidence of fostering holistic small groups that focus on the application of Christian teaching to daily life in the family and community. The term "holistic" suggests the tendency to form wholes that are greater than the sums of their parts. The Alpha study groups were a prime example. There were the *Moms and Tots* sessions, which were initially intended for BCBC members and adherents who were willing to invite unchurched neighbours and friends. Thus young mothers were encouraged to meet one another. While highly desirable, these groups were not fully effective. *Guess who is coming to lunch*, which later continued as *Table Talk,* was meant to be another forum for discussion around the meaning of the Christian faith in daily life. Meetings for Men's Breakfast Sessions fostered strengthened relationships. Specific ministry groups, such as the choir and the Pastoral Care team, apart from the dimensions of their unique service areas, became groups for mutual support.

Loving Relationships

"Loving relationships enable people to experience authentic Christian love."

There is evidence that the members of the BCBC congregation reached out to others, within and without its fellowship, in demonstrations of genuine Christian love that cares for others, as an end in itself, and not as a means to another end. For instance, there were caring receptions at the occasion of marriages and funerals. Some members regularly provided transportation for others in need. The Service Commission offered meal support during short-term illness. When there were conflicts, members were encouraged to seek out one another to resolve the conflicts in a spirit of love. As happens in all organizations, BCBC had its share of critical spirits or unthinking gossip which impeded loving relationships. In some instances, members or adherents may have felt left out because of some hurtful experiences, which is most regrettable, and which may sometimes have resulted in people leaving the fellowship.

Summary

In summarizing the signals of health in BCBC's experience of ministry during its first twenty-five years, the words of Paul in Philippians 3: 12 come to mind: *"Not that I have already obtained this or am already perfect; but I press on to make it my own, because Christ Jesus has made me his own."*[245] Thus the BCBC congregation, during its first 25 years, had shown a vibrant and intense Christian faith in all categories of ministry, which, while no doubt leaving room for further growth, showed all the signs of a good measure of spiritual health.

Chapter 13: What Have We Learned?

Lesson 1. The first lesson is that to minister in a diverse community in terms of Christian expression, it is important to focus the church's ministry on central issues, while permitting some variations.

Lesson 2. The second and fundamental lesson which we have learned is that openness to the whole Body of Christ, in terms of membership, enriches the Christian experience of all, since the congregation is regularly exposed to the rich diversity of expression of faith.

Lesson 3. The third lesson is that while believer's baptism by immersion is not a condition of membership at BCBC, baptism by immersion is the practice at Bilberry, where health permits. Nevertheless, some members who came into the fellowship from other Christian traditions on their profession of faith in Christ, nevertheless subsequently requested believer's baptism because of their desire to have that personal Christian experience.

Lesson 4. The fourth lesson is that BCBC's linguistic and racial diversity proved to be a mutual enrichment when the French and English speaking choirs joined in special services at both congregations as well as in such evangelistic outreach ministries as on Petrie Island on Canada Day.

Lesson 5. The fifth lesson is that the encouragement of all to participate in accordance with their unique gifts and abilities in the ministry of the church, had pushed the Christian witness of the congregation far beyond its own four walls into the wider Christian and non-Christian community.

Lesson 6. The sixth lesson is that the "Partnership of Equals" was an effective way of sharing on-site resources at BCBC thus reaching out to the English and French speaking segments of the community, an arrangement that enabled the young French-speaking congregation to grow without an excessive financial burden.

Lesson 7. The seventh lesson is that the commitment to responsible church finance, permits the congregation to focus on the different areas of ministry, without dissipating its strength in an unnecessarily more complex physical infrastructure. In order to provide desirable services, such as the summer program, the church accepted partial financial support from *Ontario Works* and *Human Resources and Skills Development* (HRSDC).

Lesson 8. The eighth lesson is that intergenerational needs of the congregation can be effectively addressed through blended worship, where sometimes even older hymns can be presented in a more contemporary style, or where children participate by means of skits.

Lesson 9. The ninth lesson is that people who bring innovative approaches to ministry can be encouraged to test these over a limited timeframe, provided such ideas fit into the mission and purpose of the church.

Lesson 10. The tenth lesson is that change brings opportunities for organizational and personal growth, for renewal/refocus, and for exercising new and unused gifts. Change may bring "blood, sweat and tears" also, but is inevitable, to meet changing needs, changing times and new missions. Bilberry has changed, stretched and grown, taking new steps and taking on new initiatives, perhaps every five years since 1985. This can be both energizing and exhausting!

Chapter 14: Looking Ahead

In looking ahead, do we have a future vision or perceive new possibilities? In the past, the congregation perceived major steps: When we grow from 20 to 100, build for 200; when we grow from 100 to 200, then build for 400; then when we grow from 200 to 400, launch a new church plant. The question is when? Perhaps 10 years from now? The fundamental question is whether the earlier paradigm still holds. If not, what is it now?

The future might hold several forms of development and growth, such as:

1. At the end of the first twenty-five years of BCBC's existence, the congregation looked with great expectation to the completion of Phase IIA and to access to more ample space. This new condition should not be viewed as a grant of greater luxury, but rather as an opportunity for more effective outreach into the community, with a view to responding to unmet needs for Christian service.

2. Within the congregation, the Deacons and the Pastoral Care Team should seek opportunities for continuing growth in their intended role of targeted visitation or other form of contact, such as the use of occasional telephone calls, covering the entire church family. This is always urgent, since there is evidence that some members and adherents have left the fellowship for unknown reasons, without follow-up. This might call for a priority listing of some members and adherents for contact. No doubt, someone always knows why, but it may not be shared. Perhaps there are appropriate forms of record

keeping, follow up, big picture reassessment/retro-assessment that can be put in place. This is an aspect of how we learn and improve.

3. The BCBC leadership might explore how the preaching component, and or the holistic group approach, should be strengthened with a view to developing home congregations and/or satellites in emerging larger communities, with a view to eventually creating the conditions for new churches. Holistic groups might reach out into the community if there are unique needs to which they can respond.

4. The Teaching Commission might broaden its reach beyond the church, by encouraging members of the congregation to participate in suitable forms of distance education in Christian faith and practice.

5. The Evangelism Commission might explore more options for needs-driven evangelism, based on knowing who their neighbours are and which needs present themselves. This is particularly important as the congregation becomes aware of the broken nature of the world, which entails changing needs. The congregation could then seek to establish effective and loving relationships with their neighbours, as they reach out in the love of Christ.

6. In all areas of leadership, the music ministry included, attempts might be made to develop understudies who would be able to take over effectively, when the current leadership retires.

7. New members should not only be welcomed, but they should be offered opportunities for effective orientation, perhaps by developing and distributing a *New Member's Guide,* which might contain an historical overview.

8. As the community is getting older, BCBC will need to find more opportunities to support its and the community's seniors.

9. As the French speaking church in the Partnership of Equals continues to grow, means need to be found how to respond to increasing requirements of space.

10. To broaden BCBC's reach, awareness of its website[246] might be strengthened and broadened.

BILBERRY – *A Seed in Good Soil*

APPENDICES

Appendix A. Summary Household and Member Statistics (1984-2009)

Over the period 1984-2009, Bilberry Creek Baptist Church had ministered to 362 households, involving 975 persons, of whom 251 (25.74%) were members.

In terms of programming for ministry, it is noteworthy that:
- 105 households (29.01%) involved only one person, an adult;
- 90 households (24.86%) involved two persons, mostly couples;
- Children or young adults were involved in 167 households (43.16%).

| Description | Number of | | | | |
	Households	Persons in household	Households with members	Households without members	Members
TOTAL	362	975	166	196	251
Average		2.69			
Range		1 - 7			
Percentage			45.86%	54.14%	25.74%
one-person households	29.01%	105			
two-person households	24.86%	90			
three-person households	10.77%	39			
four-person households	21.55%	78			
five-person households	11.33%	41			
six-person households	1.93%	7			
seven-person households	0.55%	2			

Appendix B. Baptisms

Note: This appendix lists baptisms that occurred up until September 2009.

Family Name	Given Name	Month	Day	Year
Turle	Ruth	Oct	26	1986
Wehrle	Mary	Jan	17	1988
Newsham	Ted	Jan	17	1988
Newsham	Kristen	Jan	17	1988
Newsham	Curtis	Jan	17	1988
Miskowicz	Daniel	May	27	1990
Archibald	Michael	May	27	1990
Turle	Paul	May	27	1990
Oickle	Eric	May	27	1990
Zelmer	Jillian	May	27	1990
Sears	Jeff	Apr	21	1991
Dotis	Erica	Apr	21	1991
Dotis	John	Apr	21	1991
Archibald	Kelly	Jan	12	1992
Maitland	Sarah-Jane	Jan	12	1992
Allsopp	Alison	Jan	12	1992
Collar	Bradley	Jan	12	1992
Dullemond	Ruth	Jan	12	1992
Peach	Janice	Jan	12	1992
Ruiter	Beth	May	30	1993
Zelmer	Allison	May	30	1993
Hill	Jamie	May	30	1993
Dullemond	Melissa	May	30	1993
Heuttner	Jody	May	30	1993
Radford	Barry	Jun		1994
Wehrle	Eric	Jun		1994
Jen	Kim	Oct	16	1995
Guevremont-Knorr	Esther	Oct	16	1995
Angel	Scott	Oct	16	1995
Rochow	Joanne	Jun	2	1996
Lyons	Julie	Apr	19	1998
Peach	Denise	Apr	19	1998

Family Name	Given Name	Month	Day	Year
Hall	Natasha	Jun	21	1998
Rochow	David	Jul		1998
Kiar	David	Jun	6	1999
Lyons	Andrew	Jun	6	1999
Jen	Scott	Jun	6	1999
Barriault	Sarah	May	14	2000
Drewitt	Mark	May	14	2000
Bunning	Heather	Aug		2001
Ferenchik	Linda	Feb	17	2002
O'Brien	Louis	Feb	17	2002
O'Brien	Heather	Feb	17	2002
O'Brien	Cameron	Feb	17	2002
O'Shaughnessy	Erin	Feb	17	2002
Lyons	Ron	Mar	30	2003
Camire	Claire	Mar	30	2003
Martin	Joan	Aug	17	2003
Martin	Nicolas	Aug	17	2003
Durham	Doug			
Travers-Collar	Michelle-Ann	Nov	16	2003
Chomcey	Jennifer	Nov	16	2003
Chomcey	Melody	Feb	15	2004
Rochow	Andrea	Feb	15	2004
Jefferies	Mark	May		2004
Miskowitz	David	May		2004
Barriault	Kimberly	Oct	17	2004
Barriault	Paul	Oct	17	2004
Plows	Emilie	Mar	27	2005
Cooper	Connie	May		2005
Bunning	Mark	Jul	24	2005
Atallah	Elie	Oct	16	2005
Atallah	Elianne	Oct	16	2005
Dupuis	Daniel	Nov	20	2005
Arrand	Stefanie			2005
Brett	Wendy	Feb	26	2006

Family Name	Given Name	Month	Day	Year
Hughes	Cheryl	Nov		2006
Moke	Susan	Aug	27	2006
Wade	Lorraine	Jun	12	2008
Messer	Jennifer	Jan	3	2008
Somers	James	Jan	3	2008
Dupuis	Terri	Jan	20	2008
Dupuis	Peter	Jan	20	2008
McClure	Sharon	May	4	2008
Yuma-Morisho	Andrea	Jan	27	2008
Baxter	Roxanne	Oct	11	2008
McClure	Linda	Oct	11	2008
Cavey	Michael	Aug	2	2009
McCulloch	Sue	Apr	12	2009

BILBERRY – *A Seed in Good Soil*

Appendix C: In Memoriam

The BCBC congregation fondly remembers:

Barry Moss
13 October 1959 to 5 May 1989

Antonine Garnier
1993

169

Joanne Guitard

Austin Moss
1 April 1932 to 12 September 1999

Yvon E. Lanctin
3 July 1925 to 9 June 2001

Gertrude Cunningham-Latondresse
3 September 1912 to 9 June 2005

Harold & Merle Birch
Merle: 2 December 1928 to 2 February 2003
Harold: 16 November 1924 to 25 October 2007

Joan Martin
3 December 1924 to 21 July 2005

Alan Grant Birch
12 December 1931 to 13 September 2006

J. Campbell Stephens
25 October 1937 to 1 February 2009

Appendix D: Order of Service from First Public Service (23 September 1984)

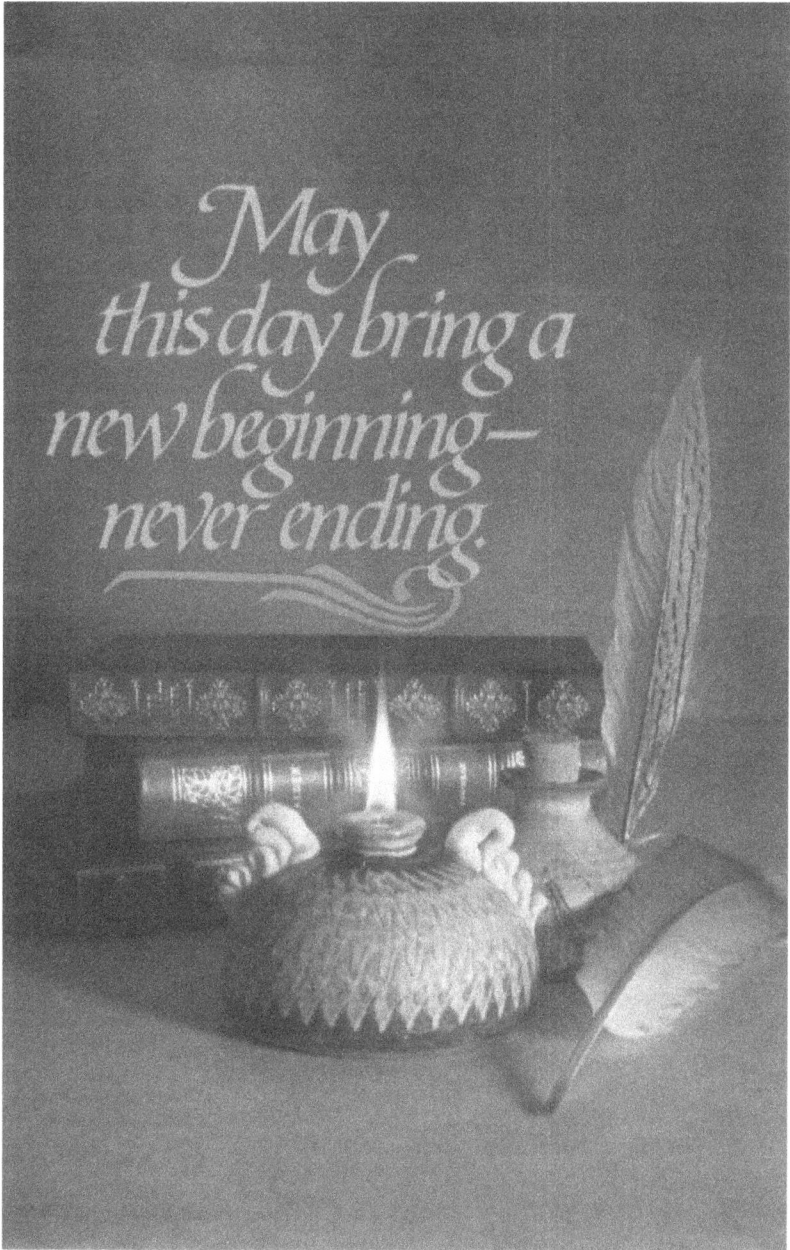

May this day bring a new beginning— never ending.

BILBERRY CREEK BAPTIST CHURCH

meeting at

Dunning-Foubert Elementary School
1610 Prestwick Drive, Queenswood Heights
Orleans, Ontario

SUNDAY, 23 SEPTEMBER 1984

18:30

ORDER OF SERVICE

Piano Prelude

Welcome and Announcements

Call to Worship (In unison)   The Hymnal No. 611

Prayer of Approach

Hymn   "Praise, My Soul, The King Of Heaven"   138

Hymn   "Great Is Thy Faithfulness"   154

Scripture Reading: Luke 19: 11-27; 17: 20-21

Solo   "The Way That He Loves"   W. Elmo Mercer

Evening Prayer

Hymn   "Open My Eyes, That I May See"   433

Sermon   "The Coming Of The Kingdom"

Silent Prayer

Hymn   "Where Cross The Crowded Ways Of Life"   507

Offering

Offertory Music

Offertory Hymn "Bless Thou The Gifts"   597

Hymn "The Day Thou Gavest, Lord, Has Ended"   144

Benediction

Piano Postlude

*   *   *   *   *

Group Discussion   (Help Yourself To A Coffee)

*   *   *   *   *

Tonight's service is the first public meeting of this church. The service is led by the Rev. Gunter Rochow, a resident of Cumberland and a prospective charter member of this congregation. The pianist is Mrs. Bonnie Maitland and the soloist Mr. Austin Moss. The Sunday School is being led by Mrs. Lisee Kiar and by Mrs. Miriam Sears.

BILBERRY CREEK BAPTIST CHURCH is affiliated with the Baptist Convention of Ontario and Quebec and with the Canadian Baptist Federation. It is sponsored by the Ottawa Baptist Association.

The BAPTIST WOMEN WORLD DAY OF PRAYER will be held at Eastview Baptist Church, Monday, November 5th, 10 a.m. Babysitting will be available. All are welcome.

A CHOIR is to be formed shortly. Interested persons may contact Mr. Austin Moss at 824-7601.

NEXT SUNDAY: The service will be led by the Rev. Neil Hunter, the Minister of Bethany Baptist Church, Nepean.

If you desire more information about this church or require a pastoral service, please speak to the officiating minister or tear off this portion and leave it on the offering plate.

NAME: TELEPHONE:

NOTES

[1] These include Mark Parent's report to Archie Goldie (BCOQ Department of Ministry), the Minutes/Resolution of the Ottawa Baptist Association (OBA) to proceed with church extension in the Orleans area, as well as certain early BCBC annual and commission reports, including financial and membership data.

[2] Acts 16:9.

[3] BCBC. Church Bulletin for the opening service, September 23, 1984.

[4] In December 1984, Neil Hunter sent a Christmas letter to the congregation signed "for the Support and Steering Committee".

[5] BCBC, Support and Steering Committee, June 1985. The members of the SSC then were Don Collar, Neil Hunter, Lo-Sun Jen, Lisee Kiar, Colin McGregor, Austin Moss, Gunter Rochow, Carl Sears, Richard (Chairman) and Helen Turle, and Douglas Warnock.

[6] BCBC. Support and Steering Committee Minutes, June 1985.

[7] BCBC Special Meeting, January 22,1985. Members present: Sheila Davenport, Bert de Roo (Chairman), Rev. Neil Hunter, Lo-Sun Jen, Lisee Kiar, Austin Moss, Gunter and Reinhilde Rochow, Carl Sears, Richard Turle, Darlene Tytula, Douglas Warnock, and, as special guest, the Rev. Don Collar.

[8] BCBC. Order Of Service. Among other participants, Mr. George Baker, as Moderator, brought greetings on behalf of the Ottawa Association of Baptist Churches.

[9] *Express*, 15 mai 1985, p. 5.

[10] BCBC. 1987 Annual Report of the Support and Steering Committee. Members from outside of the congregation were: Dr. Keith Cooney; Rev. Bert de Roo; Rev. Neil Hunter; Mr. Colin McGregor; and Mr. Douglas Warnock. Members from within the congregation were: Dr. Lo-Sun Jen; Mrs. Lisee Kiar; Mr. Austin Moss; Rev. Gunter Rochow; Mr. Carl Sears; and Mr. Richard Turle (Chairman). The Report also recognized as members of the Constitution Committee: Don Collar; Austin Moss; Fern Richardson; and Gunter Rochow.

[11] G. R. Beasley Murray. Baptism in the New Testament. McMillan & Co Ltd. London, 1962, 424 pp.

[12] William R. Wood, Ä Study of Church Membership in relation Baptism" (McMaster Divinity College History Conference, October 25-29, 1982), p. 27.

[13] BCBC. Annual Report. 1987, 3rd page.

[14] BCBC. Council Minutes, November 1996, page 4 and February 1997, page 1.

[15] BCBC. Constitution, Byelaw 3.

[16] BCBC. Constitution, Byelaw 4.

[17] Annual Program Meeting of the Bilberry Creek Baptist Church (unincorporated), followed by First meeting of the Body incorporated in Ontario, known as Bilberry Creek Baptist Church, both on June 12th, 2008.

[18] BCBC. Sunday Bulletin, January 24, 2009.

[19] BCBC. Council, October 1989.

[20] BCBC. *Celebrate our Journey* [Annual Report] 1989, page 4.

[21] BCBC. Annual Report. 1996, 3rd page.

[22] BCBC. Annual Report. 1997, pages 5, 7th and 11th.

[23] BCBC. *Creating the Future: Bilberry and Église Évangélique in Partnership – A discussion document on recommendation from the Phase II Committee.* January 2003, page 3.

[24] "Our Story", presented at the BCBC 24th Anniversary services gives January 1998 as the starting point for the French ministry. On the other hand, the BCBC Sunday bulletin of February 9, 1997 announced the beginning of French services for March 2, 1997.

[25] BCBC. Constitution, Appendix D: Bilberry Creek Baptist Church and Église Évangelique Baptiste D'Orléans Covenant.

[26] BCBC. Annual Report. 1989, 7th page.

[27] BCBC. Annual Report. 2001, page 1

[28] BCBC. Annual Report. 2001, page 1

[29] BCBC. Challenger, June 1989.

[30] BCBC. Annual Report 1989, page 2.

[31] BCBC. Annual Report. 1989, 7th page.

[32] BCBC. Annual Report. 1989, 7th page.

[33] BCBC. Annual Report. 1989, 7th page.

[34] BCBC. Challenger, April 1990.

[35] BCBC. Annual Report. 1991, 9th page.

[36] BCBC. Annual Report. 1994, 7th page.

[37] BCBC. Challenger, volume 6, number 4 and volume 7, number 1.

[38] BCBC. Annual Report. 1994, 7th page; also Annual Report 1999, 16th page.

[39] BCBC. Council Meeting, June 1995 and email from Don Collar to Gunter Rochow dated August 15, 2009.

[40] BCBC. Extraordinary General Meeting, March 7, 1992.

[41] BCBC. Annual Report 1997, p. 14.

[42] BCBC. Annual Report. Trustee Report, June 1993, 2nd page. The same idea was also reflected in BCBC Annual Report 1994, 7th page.

[43] Source. Richard Turle.

[44] BCBC. Annual Report. 2004, 13th page.

[45] BCBC. Challenger, February 2005, April 2005 and September 2006.

[46] BCBC. Annual Report 2008.

[47] The members of the Phase II Committee were: Bob Zelmer , Mary Wherle , Brad Collar, Bing Hum and Richard Turle. Louis   OBrien managed the financial aspects along with Karen Arbour.

[48] BCBC. Challenger, Volume 6, Number 2, August 1993

[49] BCBC. Annual Report. 14th page.

[50] BCBC. Challenger, December 2005.

[51] BCBC. Annual Report. 2003, 11th page.

[52] BCBC. Annual Report. 2001, Annual Budget Meeting, February 3, 2001, 1st page.

[53] BCBC. Challenger, volume 5, number 1 on Phase I funding.

[54] BCBC. Council Minutes, September 2008.

[55] Don and Cathy Collar have in their possession a re, according of this televised service.

[56] Greater Orleans Ministerial Association. Names and Addresses of members (those who attend).

[57] *Presbyterian Record*, December 01, 2001(http://s.rochow.info/bilberry-01)

[58] http://www.machzikeihadas.com/

[59] http://www.bilberry.org/

[60] BCBC. Council Minutes. September 11, 2002, Jillian Zelmer's letter to the Search Committee.

[61] BCBC. Council Minutes. October 2, 2002, 2nd page.

[62] BCBC. Annual Report. 2003, Jillian Zelmer's Report, page 2.

[63] BCBC. Annual Report. 2008-2009.

[64] BCBC. Annual Report. 2004, 14th page.

[65] BCBC. Council Minutes. September 14, 2006, page 3.

[66] BCBC 2008 Annual General Meeting. Book of Reports, third page.

[67] BCBC. Annual Report. 2007.

[68] Mary Payne. "Pastoral care program initiated in Orleans", *Express,* March 26, 1986.

[69] BCBC. Council Minutes, March 1996.

[70] Pastoral Care Team Programme January – March 1986, held on Monday evenings at St. Joseph's Parish Church.

[71] BCBC. Annual Report. 2008, 9th page.

[72] BCBC Church Bulletin, September 23, 1984

[73] The BCBC Church Bulletin, Easter 1988, is the first extant evidence of the existence of a choir.

[74] The Commission's report was referenced in the Annual Report for 1987-1988 and was received at the Annual Program Meeting on May 29, 1988.

[75] Worship Commission Report 1996-1997, appended to the BCBC Annual Program Report 1997.

[76] BCBC, Annual Report 1998-1999, page 3.

[77] Teaching Commission Report 1992-1993, submitted to the 1993 Annual Program Meeting.

[78] BCBC Church Bulletin, Father's Day June 15, 1986.

[79] The Challenger, April 2006, page 5.

[80] BCBC Church Bulletin for September 23 and 30, 1984.

[81] BCBC Church Bulletin for September 30, 1984.

[82] BCBC Church Bulletin, March 1, 1985.

[83] BCBC Church Bulletin, June 9, 1985.

[84] BCBC Church Bulletins, September 8, 1985 and September 22, 1985, Anniversary Sunday [erroneously dated "Oct" 22, 1985].

[85] BCBC Church Bulletin, September 22, 1985

[86] BCBC. Council Minutes, May 1, 2002.

[87] Source of date of formal recognition: Richard Turle.

[88] BCBC. Challenger. Evangelism Update. December 2007.

[89] BCBC. Letter from The Mission Commission. Short-Term Missions: Are you interested? (2004)

[90] BCBC. Council Minutes. March 2000.

[91] BCBC. Annual Report. Deacons's Report for 2001-2002, 1st page.

[92] Heather Bunning. Letter to supporters, describing Tanzania experience. (undated).

[93] Heather Bunning. Invitation to partner for her work with Campus Crusade for Christ (2004).

[94] Joanna Demers. "A Glimpse of God's goodness in Sherkole", West Ethiopia (August 2008).

[95] BCBC. Council Minutes, April 2006.

[96] BCBC. Challenger. „Growing in Grace". December 2007.

[97] Jillian Zelmer. Letter to supporters. (March 1, 2002).

[98] BCBC. Challenger, 2006, pp. 1-2.

[99] BCBC. Challenger, December 1998.

[100] BCBC. Annual Report. 1994, 16th page.

[101] BCBC. Challenger. March 1989.

[102] BCBC. Challenger. Evangelism Update. December 2007.

[103] BCBC. Challenger. September 2006, p. 5.

[104] BCBC. Challenger. Evangelism Update. December 2007. Also, BCBC Annual Report, 2006-2007.

[105] In favour:

- http://s.rochow.info/bilberry-02;
- http://s.rochow.info/bilberry-03;
- http://s.rochow.info/bilberry-04; and
- http://s.rochow.info/bilberry-05

Contrary:

- http://s.rochow.info/bilberry-06;
- http://s.rochow.info/bilberry-07; and
- http://s.rochow.info/bilberry-08

[106] BCBC. Annual Report. 2007.

[107] BCBC. Sunday Bulletin, August 16, 2009.

[108] BCBC. Annual Report. 1988, 6th page.

[109] BCBC. Council, December 1992 and March 1993.

[110] BCBC. Annual Report. 1997, 6th and 13th pages.

[111] BCBC. Challenger. Christmas 1997.

[112] BCBC. Council Minutes, September 1999 and Annual Report, 2001, page 3.

[113] Louis Nguyen, July 3, 2009. Slightly edited from email sent by Douglas Rochow on February 5, 2012.

[114] BCBC. Council Minutes, September 1999.

[115] BCBC. Annual Program Meeting, 16 June 2001, 1st page.

[116] BCBC. Council Minutes, April 2002 and Challenger, Easter 2002.

[117] BCBC. Annual Program Report 2002, page 3.
[118] Email to Gunter Rochow, February 4, 2012.
[119] BCBC. Annual Report 1990, 9th page.
[120] Pittston United Church Anniversary. Church Bulletin, May 29, 1988.
[121] South Gower Baptist Church, Order of Service, November 5, 1989.
[122] BCBC. Annual Report. 1998, 26th page ff.
[123] Email to Gunter Rochow, February 4, 1912.
[124] Email to Gunter Rochow, February 4, 1912.
[125] Email to Gunter Rochow, February 4, 1912.
[126] Email to Gunter Rochow, February 4, 1912.
[127] BCBC. Annual Report. 1997, 16th page.
[128] BCBC. Annual Report. 2001, 12th page.
[129] BCBC. Annual Report. 2004, page 3.
[130] BCBC. Council Minutes: Nov 12, 2006.
[131] BCBC. Annual Report. 1986, 7th page.
[132] BCBC. Annual Report 1988. Fellowship Committee [sic.] Report for Planning Meeting, May 29, 1988.
[133] BCBC. Annual Report. 1988, 9th page ff.
[134] BCBC. Annual Report. 1990, 2nd page.
[135] BCBC. Annual Report. June 26, 1999, page 11.
[136] BCBC. Council Minutes. September 1999.
[137] BCBC. Annual Meeting, June 2003, "Bilberry Baptist Women" (17th page).
[138] http://www.promisekeepers.ca/pageid/12/
[139] BCBC. Annual Report. 1995, page 2 of Pastor's report.
[140] BCBC. Annual Report. 1986, 5th page.
[141] BCBC. Annual Report. 1988, 8th page.
[142] BCBC. Annual Report, 2006-2007.
[143] BCBC. Annual Report, 1988, 8th page.
[144] BCBC. Annual Report. 1986, 7th page.
[145] BCBC. Annual Report. 1990, 15th page.
[146] BCBC. Annual Report. 2004, page 4 and 18th page.
[147] BCBC. Annual Report. 1994, 12th page.
[148] BCBC. Challenger, September 2006, page 5.
[149] BCBC. Challenger. Easter Edition 1997, 4th page.
[150] BCBC. Annual Report. 2001, 14th page.
[151] BCBC. Challenger, Easter Edition 2003, 24th page.
[152] BCBC. Annual Report. 2001, 14th page.
[153] BCBC. Annual Report. 2004, 18th page.
[154] BCBC. Annual Report. 2001, 14th page.
[155] BCBC. Annual Report. 2004, 18th page.
[156] BCBC. Annual Report. 2003, 17th page.
[157] BCBC. Annual Report. 1986, 7th page.
[158] BCBC. Annual Report. 1987, 11th page.

[159] BCBC. Annual Report. 1989, 4th page;
[160] BCBC. Annual Report. 1990, 4th page.
[161] BCBC. Annual Report. 1991, 8th page.
[162] BCBC. Annual Report. 1995, 8th page.
[163] BCBC. Annual Report. 1990, 2nd page.
[164] BCBC. Annual Report. 1992-1993, 4th page.
[165] BCBC. Annual Report. 1997, 14th page.
[166] BCBC. Annual Report. 1999, 11th page.
[167] BCBC. Council Minutes, May 1990.
[168] BCBC. Annual Report. 1986, 8th page.
[169] BCBC. Annual Report. 1987, 9th page.
[170] BCBC. Annual Report. 1988, 7th page.
[171] BCBC. Annual Report. 1988, 16th page.
[172] BCBC. Annual Report. 1989, page 2.
[173] BCBC. Annual Report, 1998, 25th page.
[174] BCBC. Council Nov '99; Sep '00.
[175] BCBC. Council Sep '00.
[176] BCBC. Annual Report. 2001, page 2.
[177] BCBC. Annual Report. 1987, 8th page.
[178] BCBC. Annual Report. 1989, 3rd page.
[179] BCBC. Annual Report. 1990, 1st page of Pastor's report.
[180] BCBC. Annual Report. 1992-1993, 5th page. Also Annual Report 1994, 2nd page.
[181] BCBC. Annual Report, 1997, 18th page.
[182] BCBC. Council Minutes, October 2, 2002, 2nd page.
[183] BCBC. Annual Report. 1997, page 6.
[184] BCBC. Annual Report. Service Commission Report. 1991, 12th to 15th page.
[185] http://matthew2535network.com; BCBC Challenger, Spring 2009.
[186] BCBC. Annual Report. 1991, 12th page.
[187] BCBC. Annual Report. 1992-1993, 12th page.
[188] BCBC. Council Minutes, December 2002.
[189] BCBC. Annual Report. 1988, 5th page.
[190] BCBC. Annual Report. 1997, 15th page.
[191] BCBC. Annual Report. 1991, 19th page and 1998, 14th page.
[192] BCBC. Annual Report, June 1994, 4th page.
[193] BCBC. Annual Report, 2001, 17th page.
[194] BCBC. Annual Report. 1991, 13th page.
[195] BCBC. Annual Report. 1993, 12th page.
[196] BCBC. Annual Report. 1991-1992, 12th page.
[197] BCBC. Annual Report. 1991, 13th page.
[198] BCBC. Annual Report. 1994, 16th page.
[199] BCBC. Annual Report. 1987, 6th page.
[200] BCBC. Annual Report. 1998, 14th page.
[201] BCBC. Annual Report. 1996, 16th page.

[202] BCBC. Annual Report. 1990, 7th page.

[203] BCBC. Annual Report. 1996, 16th page.

[204] BCBC. Annual Report. 2001, 17th page.

[205] BCBC. Council Minutes, November 1999 and Annual Report 2007-2008.

[206] BCBC. Council Minutes, October 1999.

[207] BCBC. Annual Report, page 3.

[208] BCBC. *Guidelines for Sponsorship of Refugee.*

[209] BCBC. Annual Report. 1987, 5th page.

[210] BCBC. Annual Report. 1989, page 3.

[211] BCBC. Annual Report. 1989, page 5.

[212] BCBC. Annual Report. 1989, page 3.

[213] BCBC. Annual Report. 1990, 2nd page.

[214] BCBC. Council Minutes. 1990, 1st page.

[215] BCBC. Challenger, Thanksgiving 2001, Frequently Asked Questions.

[216] BCBC. Challenger, Thanksgiving 2001, Some Background on the Sponsorship of Mohamud Issa.

[217] BCBC. Annual Report. 2001. Annual Program Meeting, June 16, 2001, 1st page.

[218] BCBC. Annual Report. 2001. Annual Program Meeting, June 16, 2001, 1st page.

[219] BCBC. Challenger, April 2006, page 6.

[220] BCBC. Annual Report. 2007-2008, 19th page.

[221] BCBC. Challenger, April 1995, 4th page.

[222] BCBC. Challenger, Christmas 1995 (Community Employment Action Program, by Gunter Rochow); Michael Curran, "Take pride in success of employment action program" (Point of View), *Orleans Weekly Journal*, February 3, 1996, page 6; and Laurie McBurney, "Orléans churches employment program spreads across Canada" (Pastor's Perspective), *Orleans Weekly Journal*, February 3, 1996, page 8.

[223] Cécile Gladel. "Un nouveau service francophone pour les sans-emploi", *L'Express*, 6 février 1996, p. 3. BCBC. Challenger, Easter 1996.

[224] BCBC. Council Minutes, November 5, 1996, page 2/4.

[225] "Public Service Sees Biggest Staffing Squeeze Since 1990s" The Ottawa Citizen, December 28, 2010.

[226] Bert Hill. "No Work, no hope: 40,000 in region give up job search", *The Ottawa Citizen*. February 13, 1996, pp. A1 and A2.

[227] Darlene Chhangur. "Churches play key role in business sector: Local Churches Unite to Help Unemployed Back on their Feet", *The Ottawa Times*, October 1995, page 8.

[228] *Cumberland Communiqué*, October 1995, page 13.

[229] Bob Harvey. "Compassion moves churches to job-training", *The Ottawa Citizen*, January 13, 1996, page C5.

[230] Bob Harvey. "Churches aid job search: Volunteer job-finders help ease unemployment stress", *The Edmonton Journal*, January 27, 1996, page B7.

[231] Bob Harvey. "Community Employment Action Program: Ottawa churches develop job project", *The Calgary Herald*, January 27, 1996

[232] Bob Harvey. "Churches start job-finding club", *The Sudbury Star*, January 20, 1996, page D6.

[233] Bob Harvey. "Churches pioneer job program", *The Toronto Star*, January 27, 1996, page L14.

[234] CBC Radio Morningside. Gunter Rochow provided this to Catherine Macklem, in a letter dated January 22, 1996.

[235] Laurie McBurney. "Orléans' churches employment program spreads across Canada", The Orleans Weekly Journal, February 3, 1996, page 8.

[236] BCBC. Challenger, Easter 1996. Vision TV, 315 Queen Street East, Toronto, Ontario, M5A 1S7; contact: Sadia Zaman.

[237] "The Community Employment Action Program – its beginnings and workings", *MacLean's Magazine*, July 1, 1996.

[238] "Job Leads Program needs your help", Kanata Jourier Standard, June 14, 1996, pp. 37-38.

[239] BCBC. Challenger, Easter 1996.

[240] BCBC. Challenger, Easter 1996.

[241] Gunter Rochow. Unpublished text of presentation to the *Rotary Club*, January 6, 1997.

[242] *The Canadian Baptist*, Winter 2000, page 7.

[243] Available on the CBOQ website (http://baptist.ca). This was presented in the BCBC Council Minutes of March 2000, as distributed by the Ottawa Baptist Association in a letter dated March 27, 2000.

[244] Don Collar. *The Word – In celebration of 25 years of ministry at Bilberry Creek Baptist Church*, 200 pp. ISBN: 979-0-9865844-0-4. Edited by: Gunter Rochow and Richard Turle.

[245] The Holy Bible: Revised Standard Version.

[246] http://bilberry.org/.